AF262897

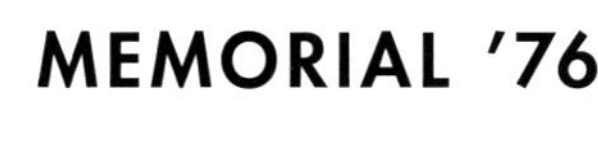
MEMORIAL '76

MEMORIAL '76

LARRY RACIOPPO

FOREWORD BY KEVIN BAKER

EMPIRE STATE EDITIONS   NEW YORK   2026

CONTENTS

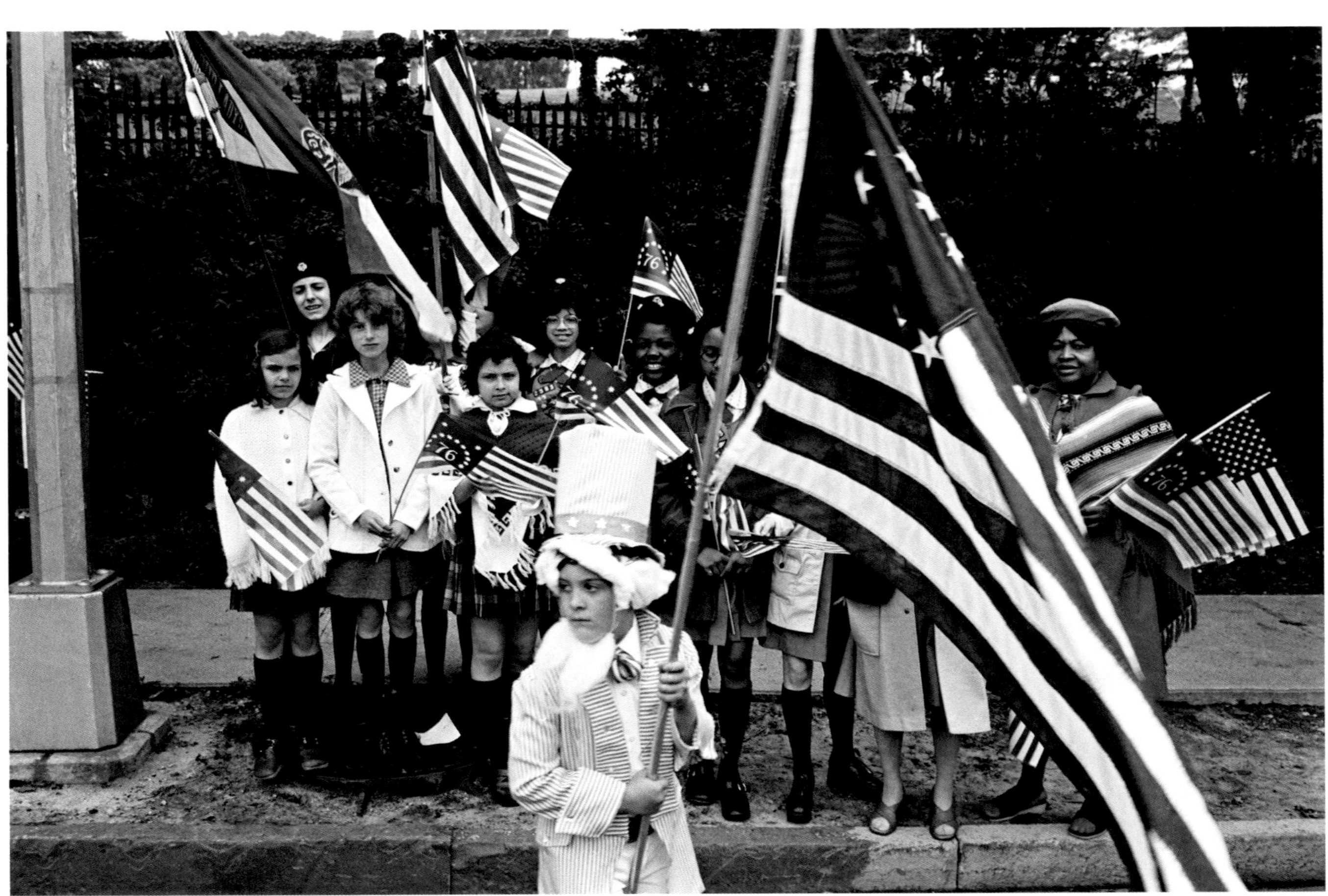

FOREWORD KEVIN BAKER

We don't often think of New York City in the 1970s as a simpler, more innocent time. But Larry Racioppo's photographs give the lie to so many of our misconceptions about that lost time and place. Here, at a bare-bones, neighborhood Memorial Day Parade in 1976, Racioppo's camera captures and enshrines that moment forever. Young people parade through a largely vanished South Brooklyn of mom-and-pop stores, fraternal clubs, auto garages, and gas stations. Young people march happily, shyly, proud of the assorted uniforms of Girl Scouts, Boy Scouts, band majorettes, and colonial re-enactors that they get to wear. Even watching members of a youthful street gang, in their jackets elaborate enough to look as though they are in a movie, seems somehow innocent under Racioppo's lens.

The entire passing scene here looks as though it could have been from a movie, or a home movie, or maybe a dream of our past. Dream-like, there is barely anybody watching from the nearly empty (but immaculately clean) streets. But those adults who are there seem happy, too, and proud, if maybe a little embarrassed to take such pleasure in such a simple, *haimishe* thing as a parade, with its marching bands and homemade floats. Here, New York's gorgeous mosaic seems to slide effortlessly into place; people of all races and backgrounds sitting outside of ethnic clubhouses, cemeteries, businesses, bars, and at home, seated in their second-story windows.

If this is not the whole story, at a time of division and turmoil in the city's history, it is the story of this moment, and it is as true as any other. Larry Racioppo's words as well as further pictures weave this small parade, this moment into the long skein of New York: the very real people, the real sacrifices that these children, these working people were celebrating in that bicentennial year. The plaques, easily missed these days, but still attached to countless churches, universities, schools, social clubs, and public buildings noting those who served, and those who died. The monuments to those who fell all across the world, but also right here in the streets of New York, the real heartland of the United States of America, where we have fought out countless times, in one way or another, just who is to be an American, and what that means.

Here is, in 1976 as today, something humble, something imperfect, but something essentially glorious. Something worth preserving. Something we will miss when it is gone.

Special Thanks

Francesca Richer for her subtle but powerful design.

Kevin Baker for his warm and perceptive essay.

The team at Fordham University Press: Fredric Nachbaur, Will Cerbone, Kathleen O'Brien-Nicholson, Katie Sweeney Parmiter, Mark Lerner, and Kem Crimmins.

My wife, Barbara Cannizzaro, for her support and insight.

And most of all to my diverse South Brooklyn neighbors whose patriotism, energy, and willingness to honor our country's fallen made this Parade possible.

"Lest we forget."

Larry R

July 2025

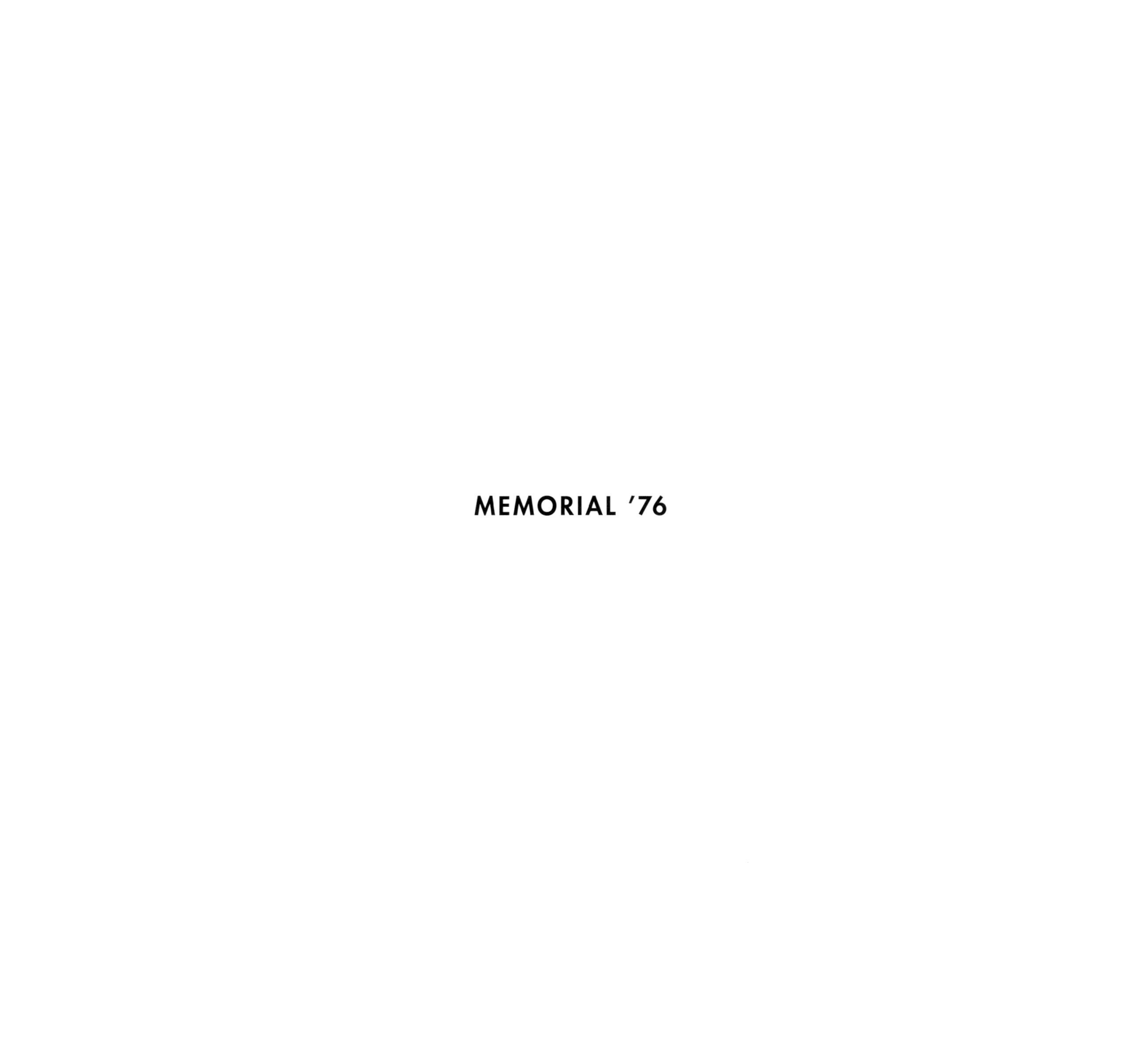

MEMORIAL '76

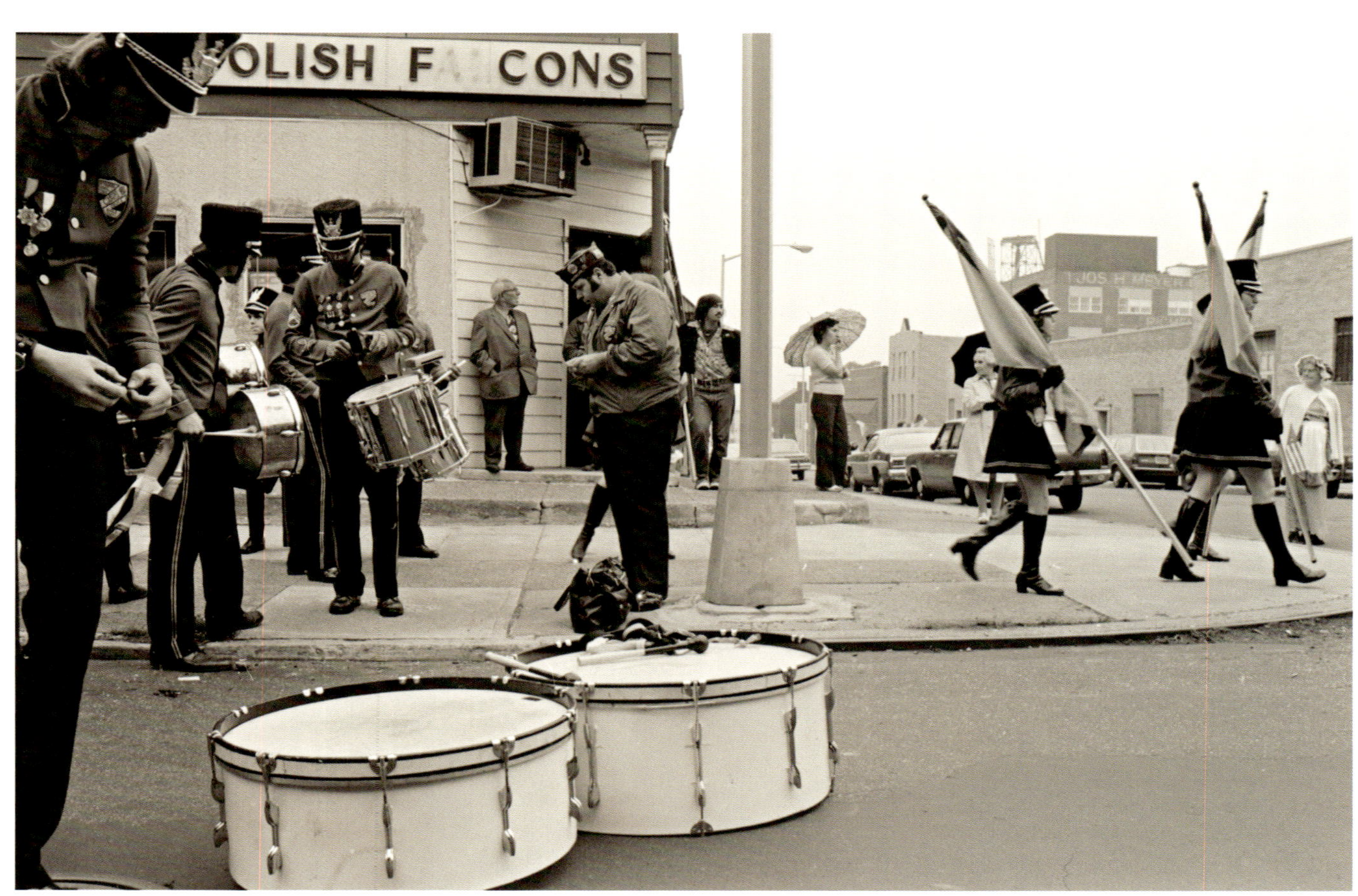
OLISH FALCONS

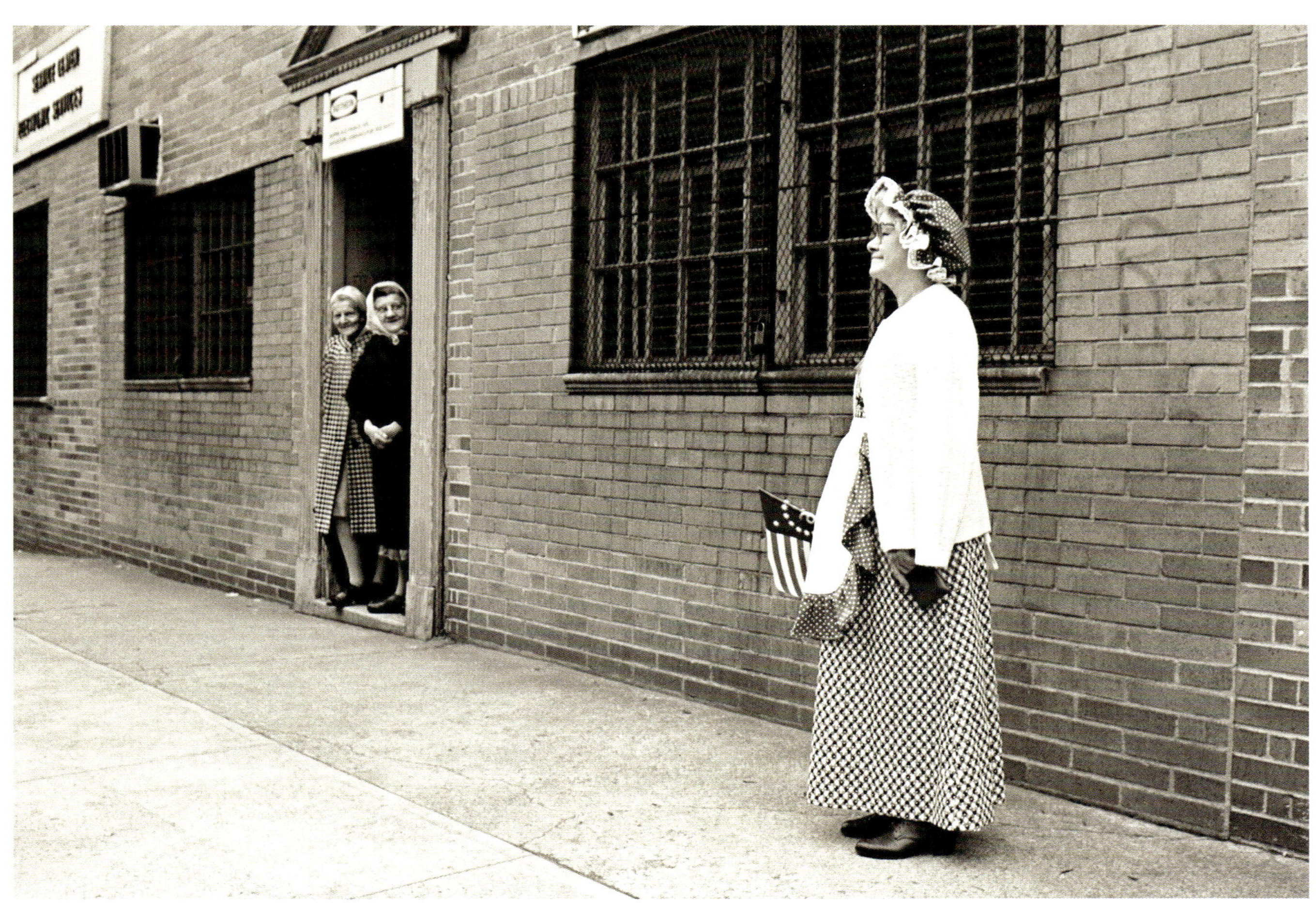

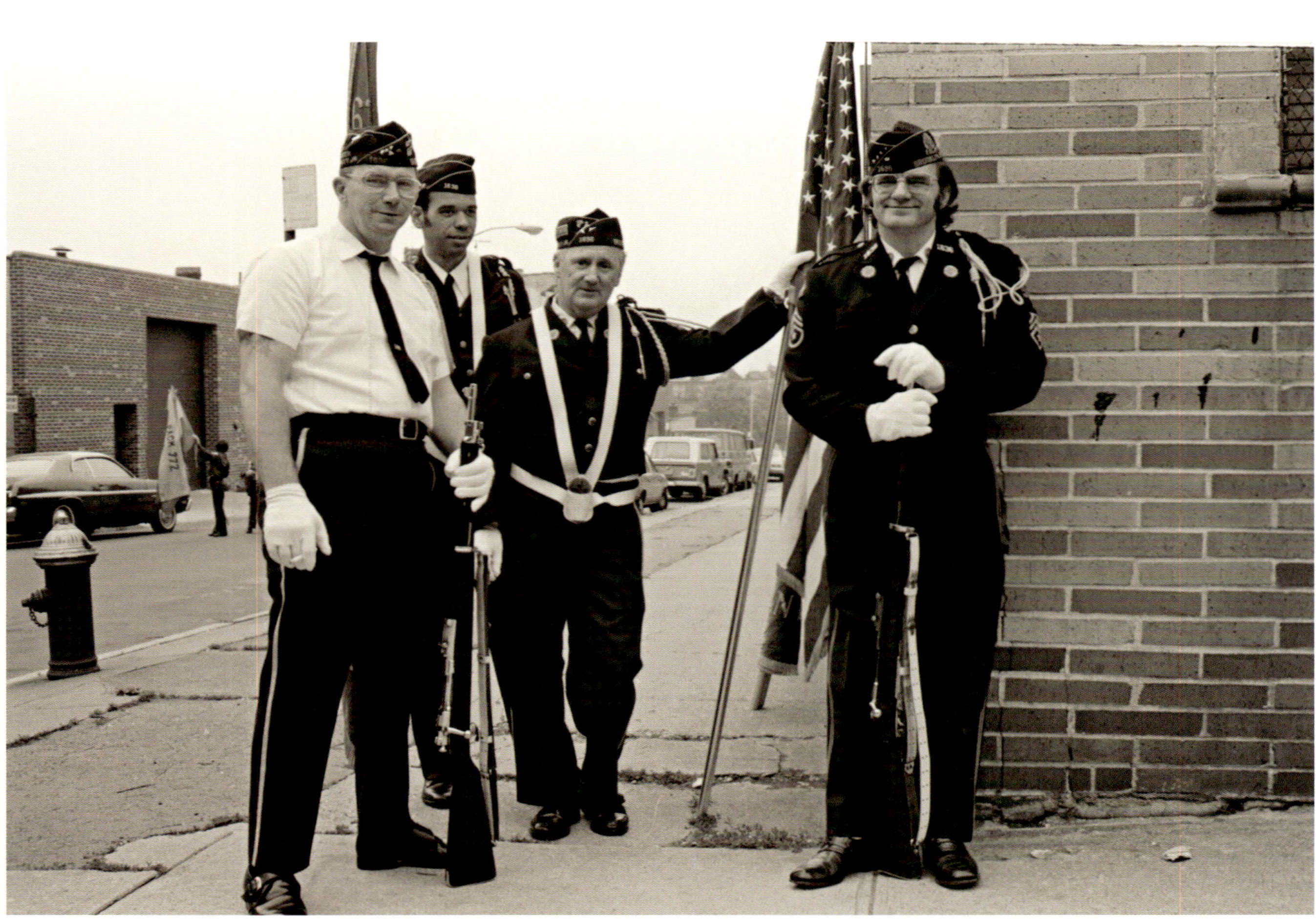

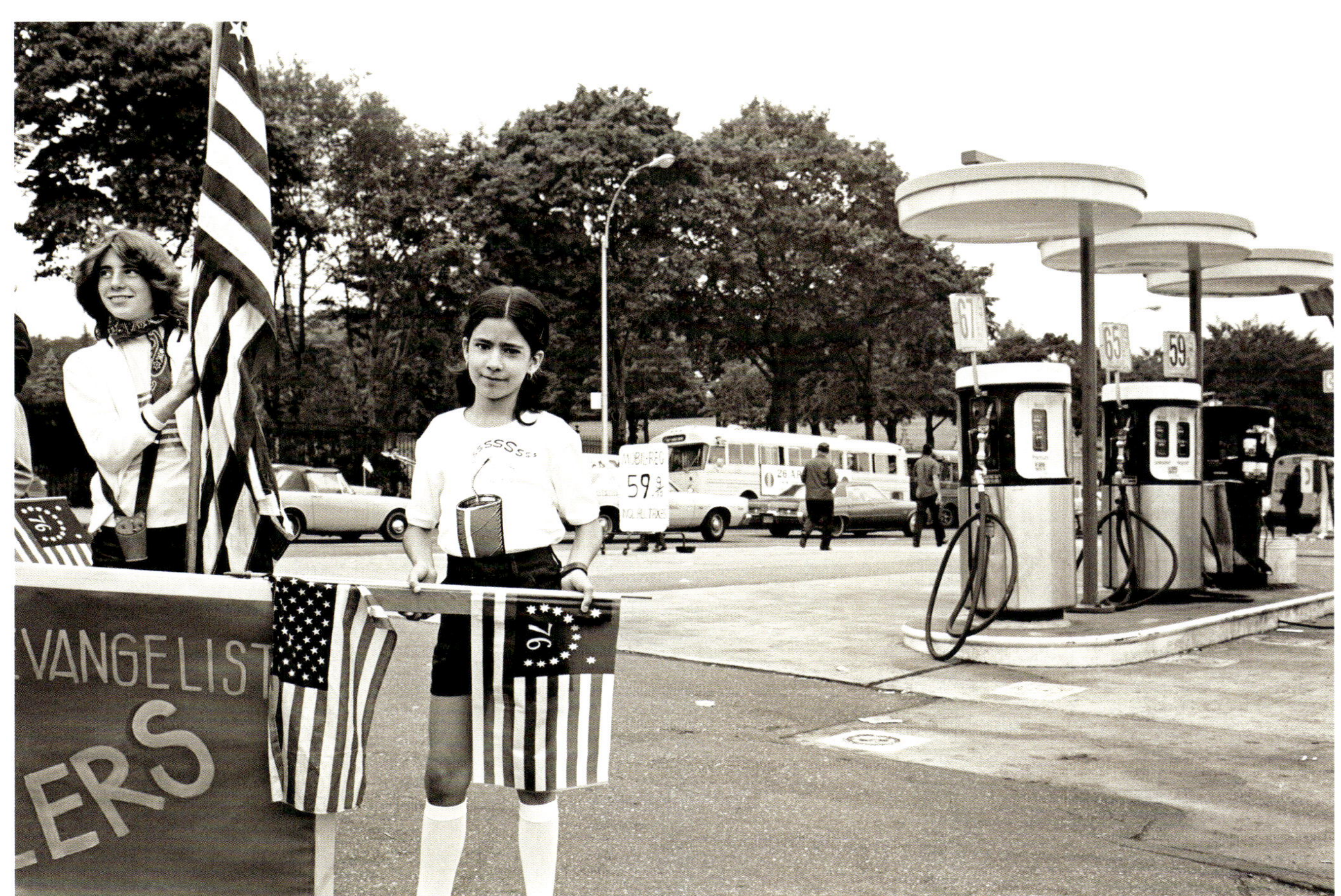
VANGELIST
ERS
76
67
65
59

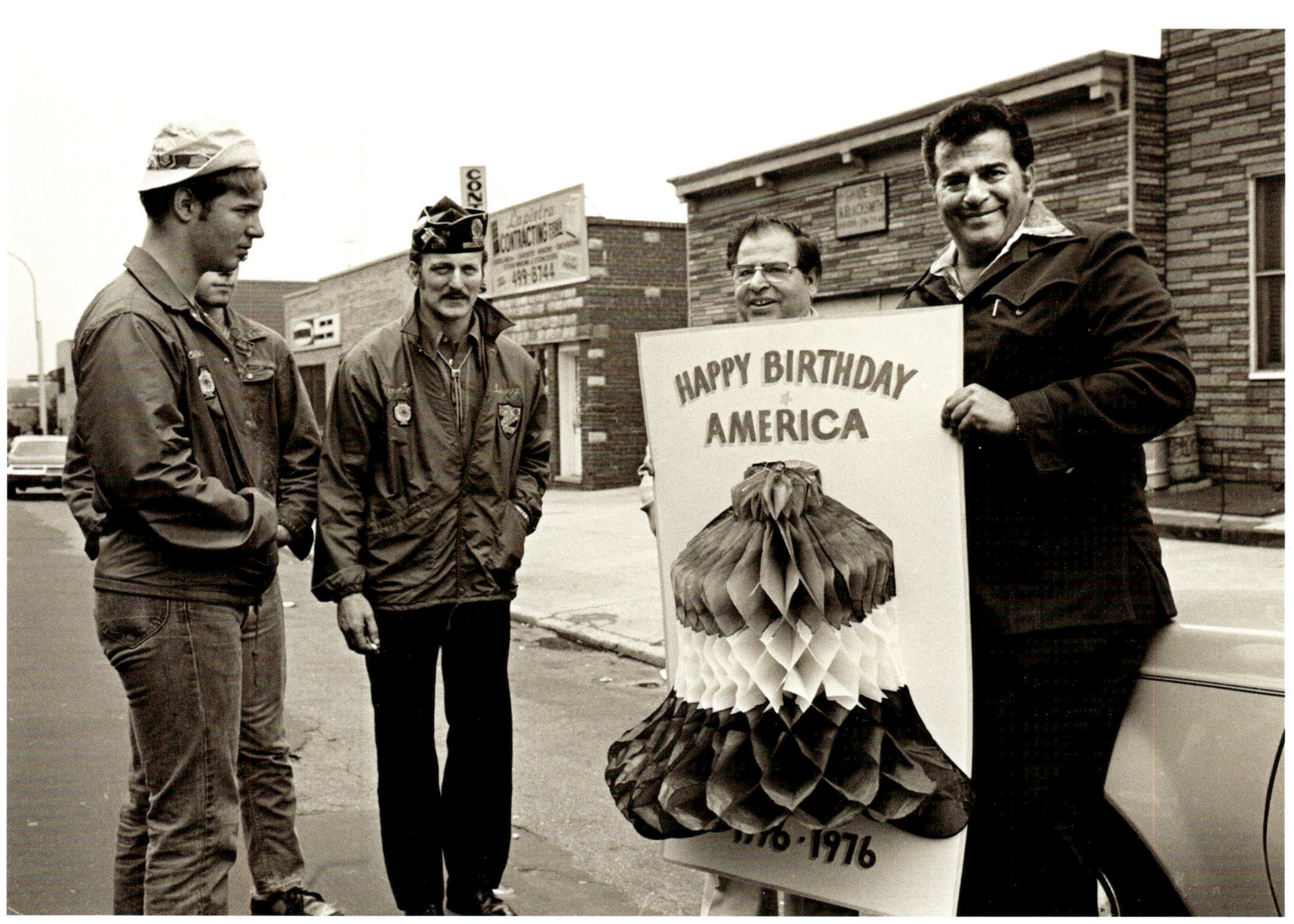
HAPPY BIRTHDAY
AMERICA
1776 · 1976

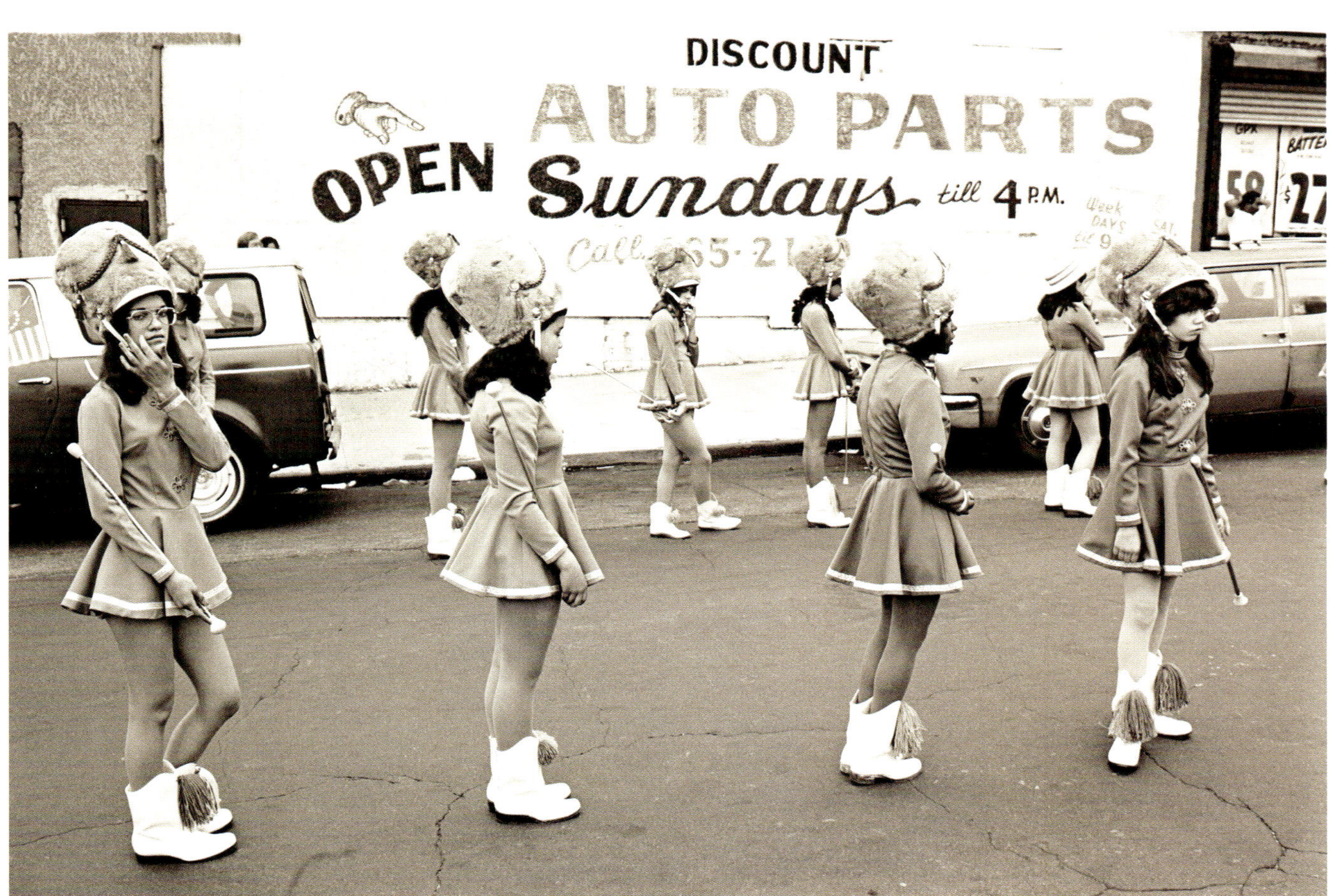
DISCOUNT
AUTO PARTS
OPEN Sundays till 4 P.M.
Call 665-21
Week DAYS
GPX
BATTE
27

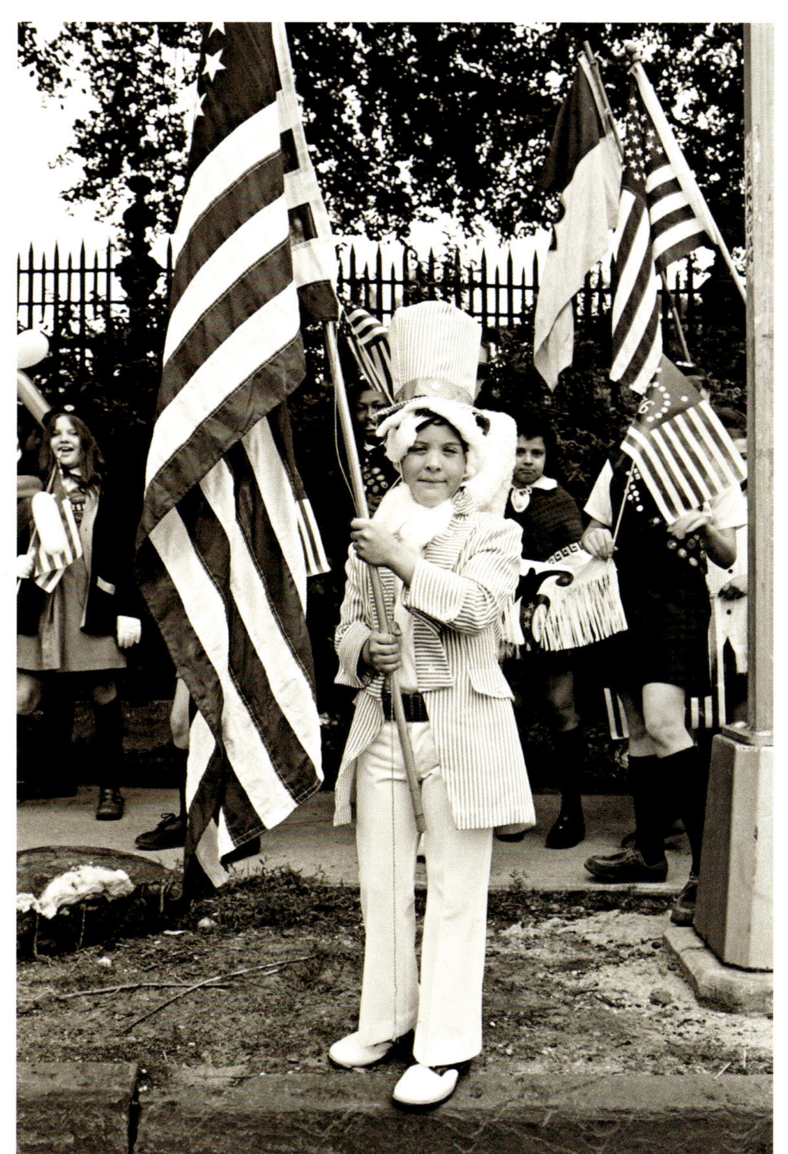

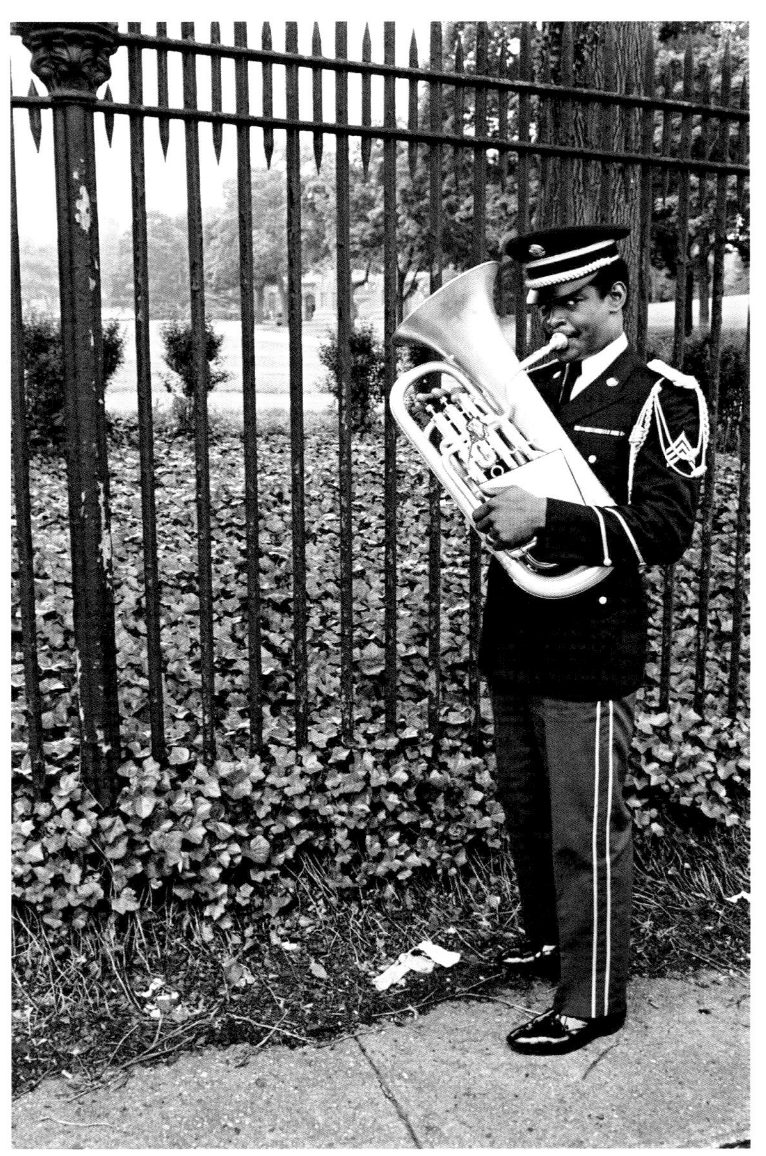

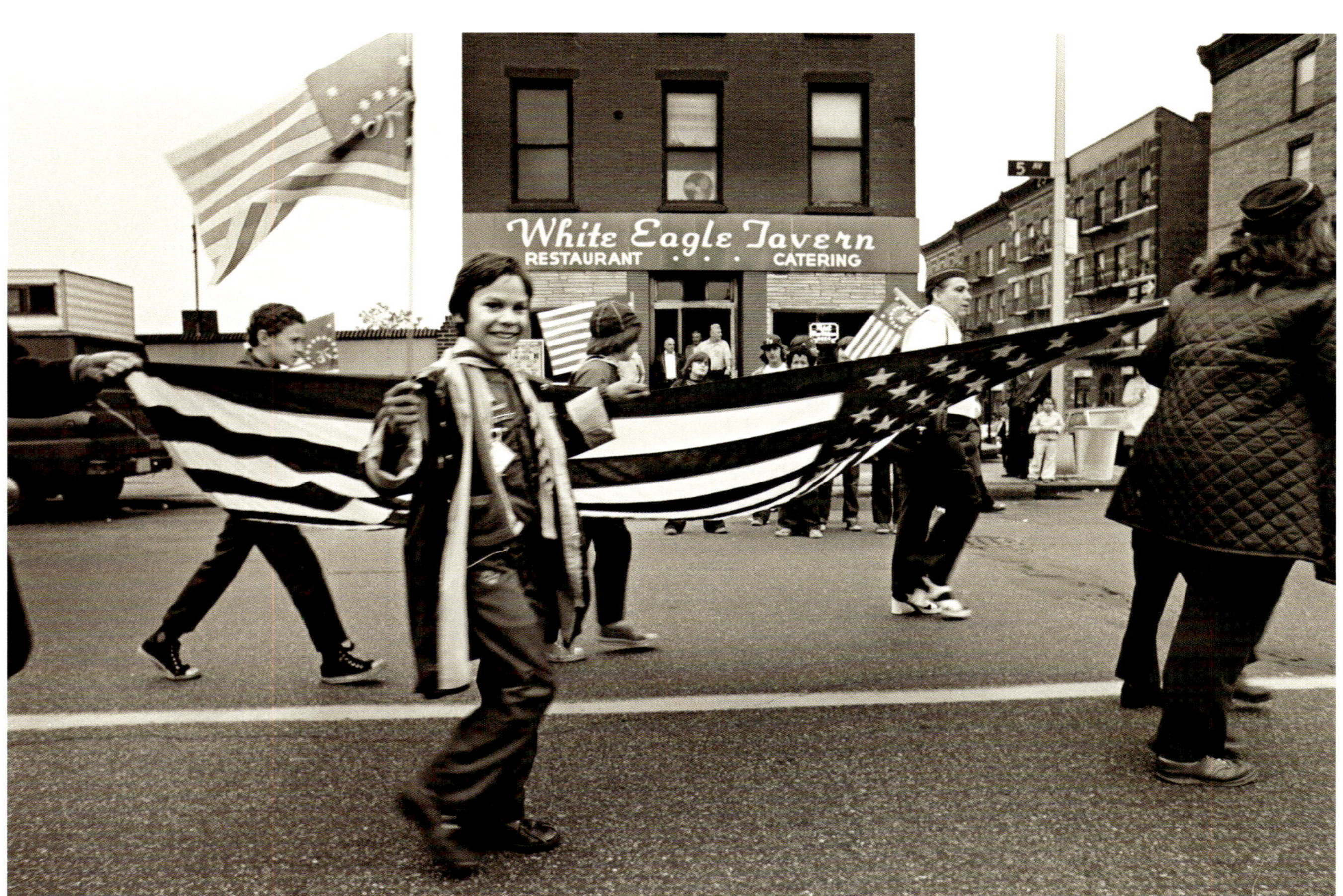
White Eagle Tavern
RESTAURANT • • • CATERING
5 AV

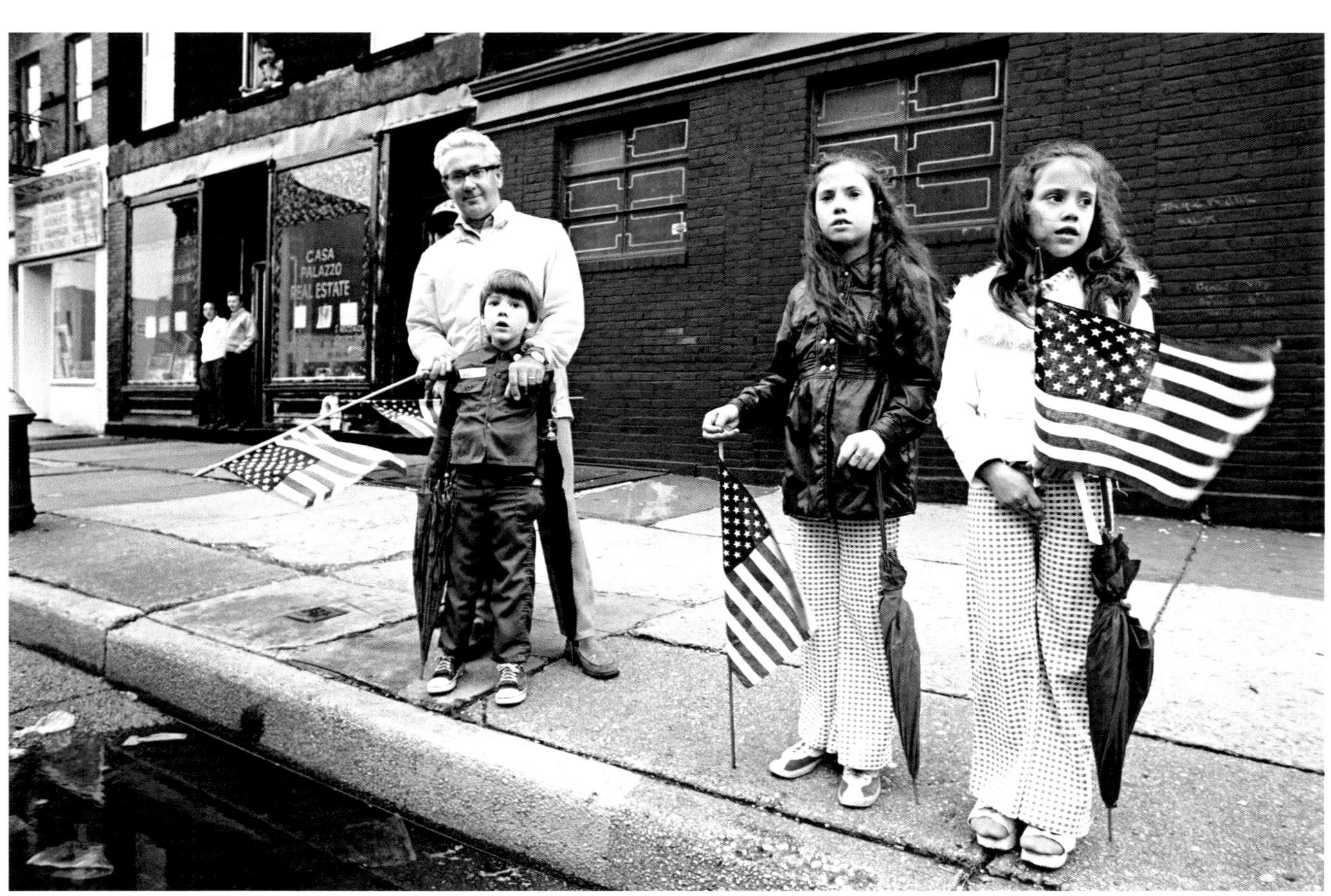

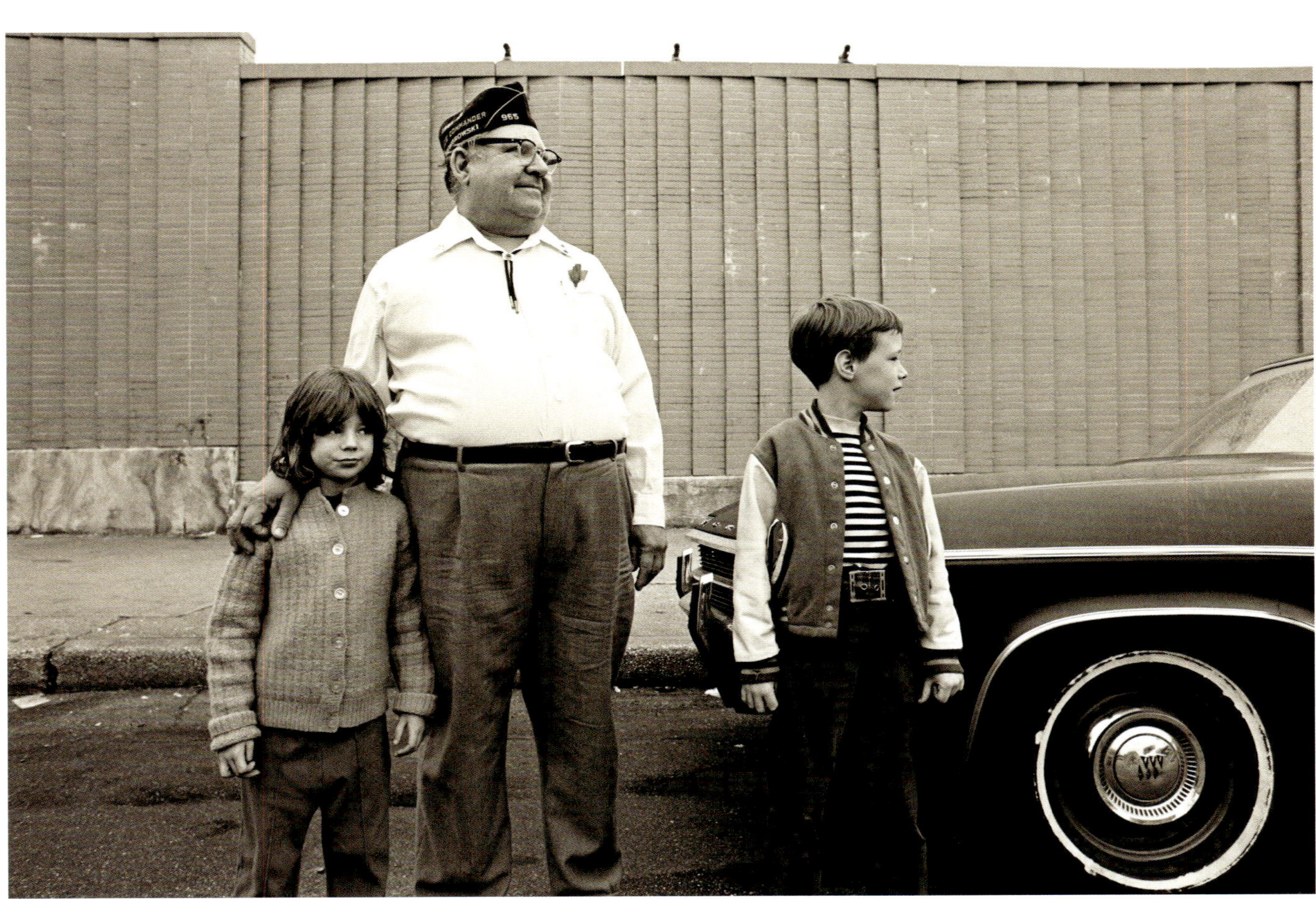

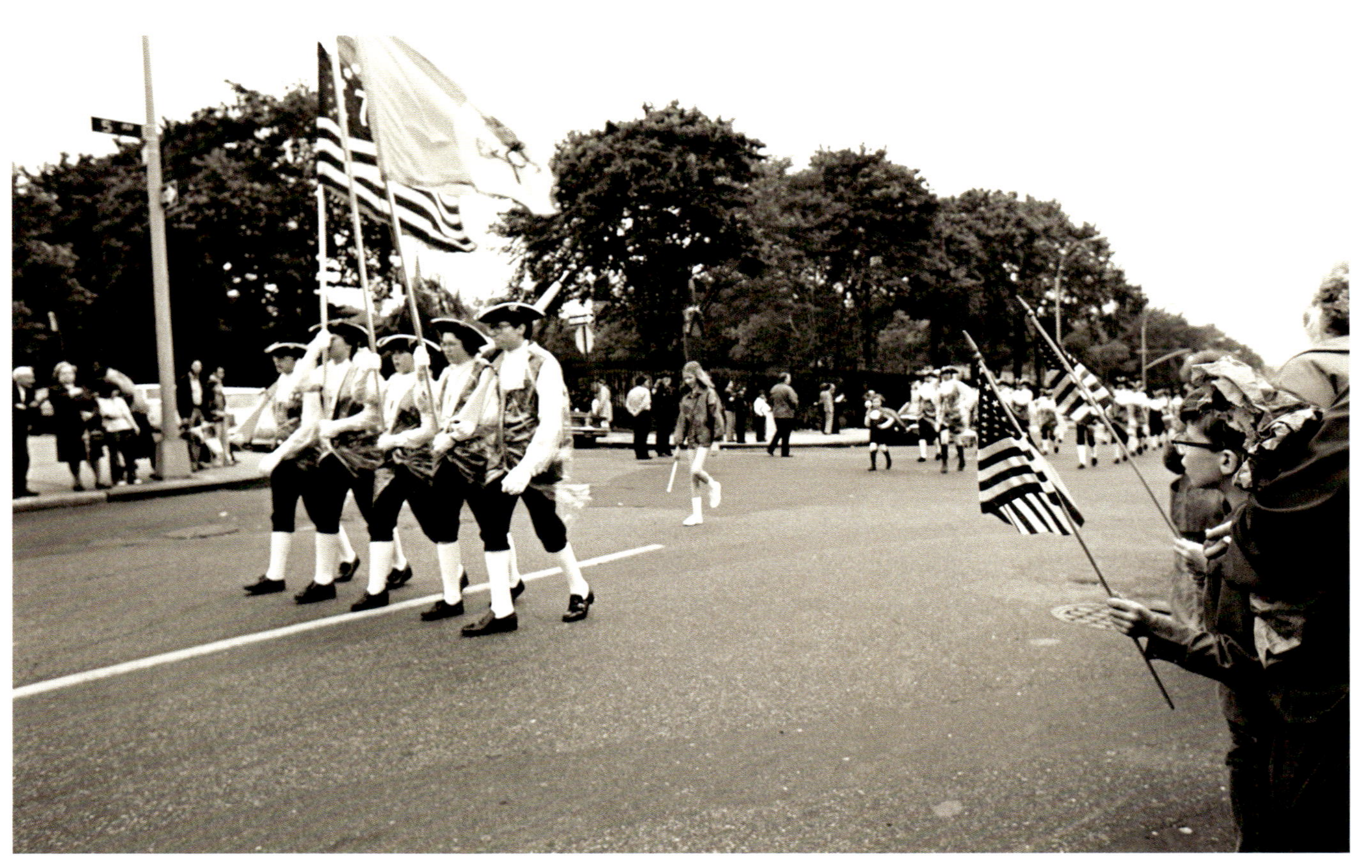

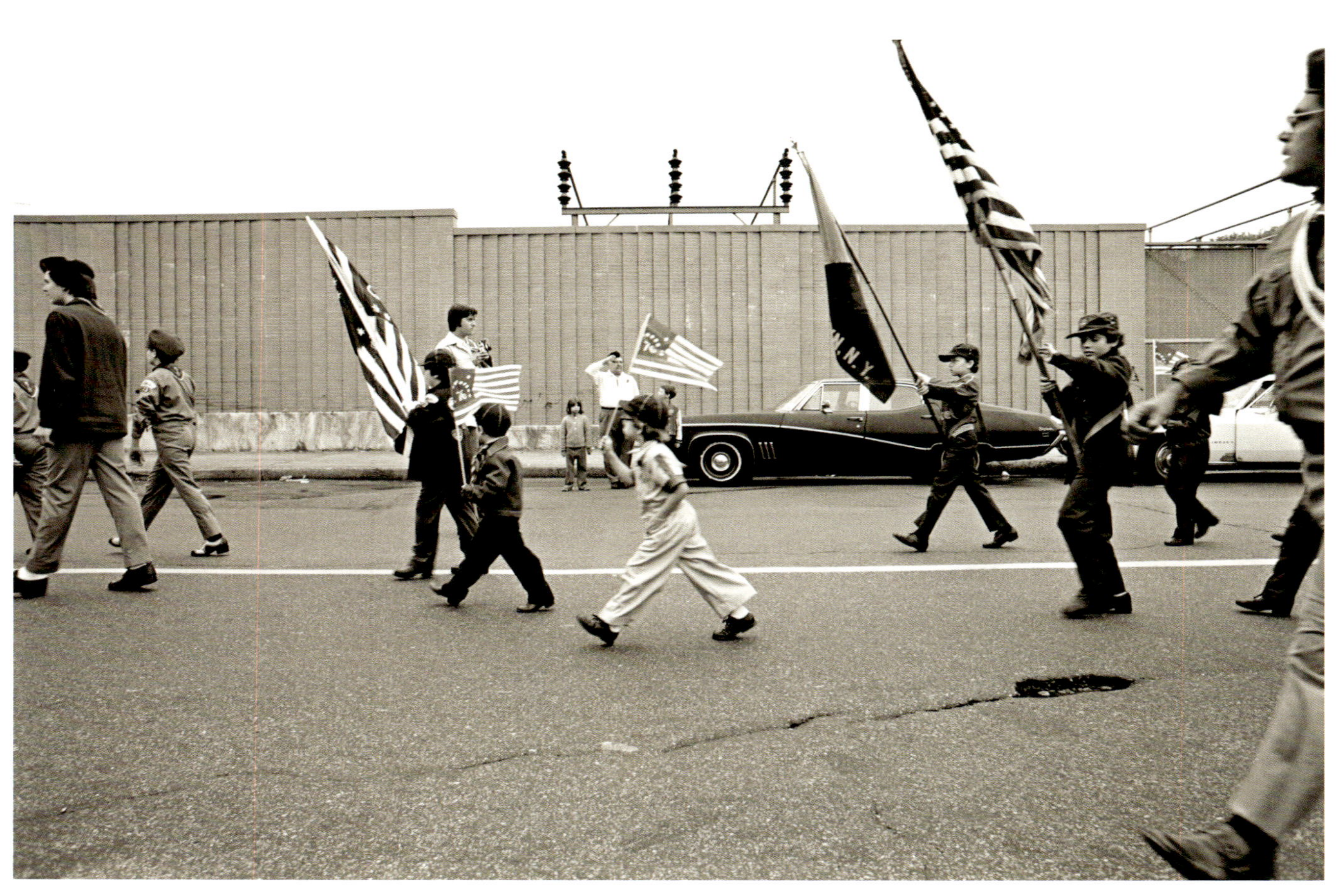

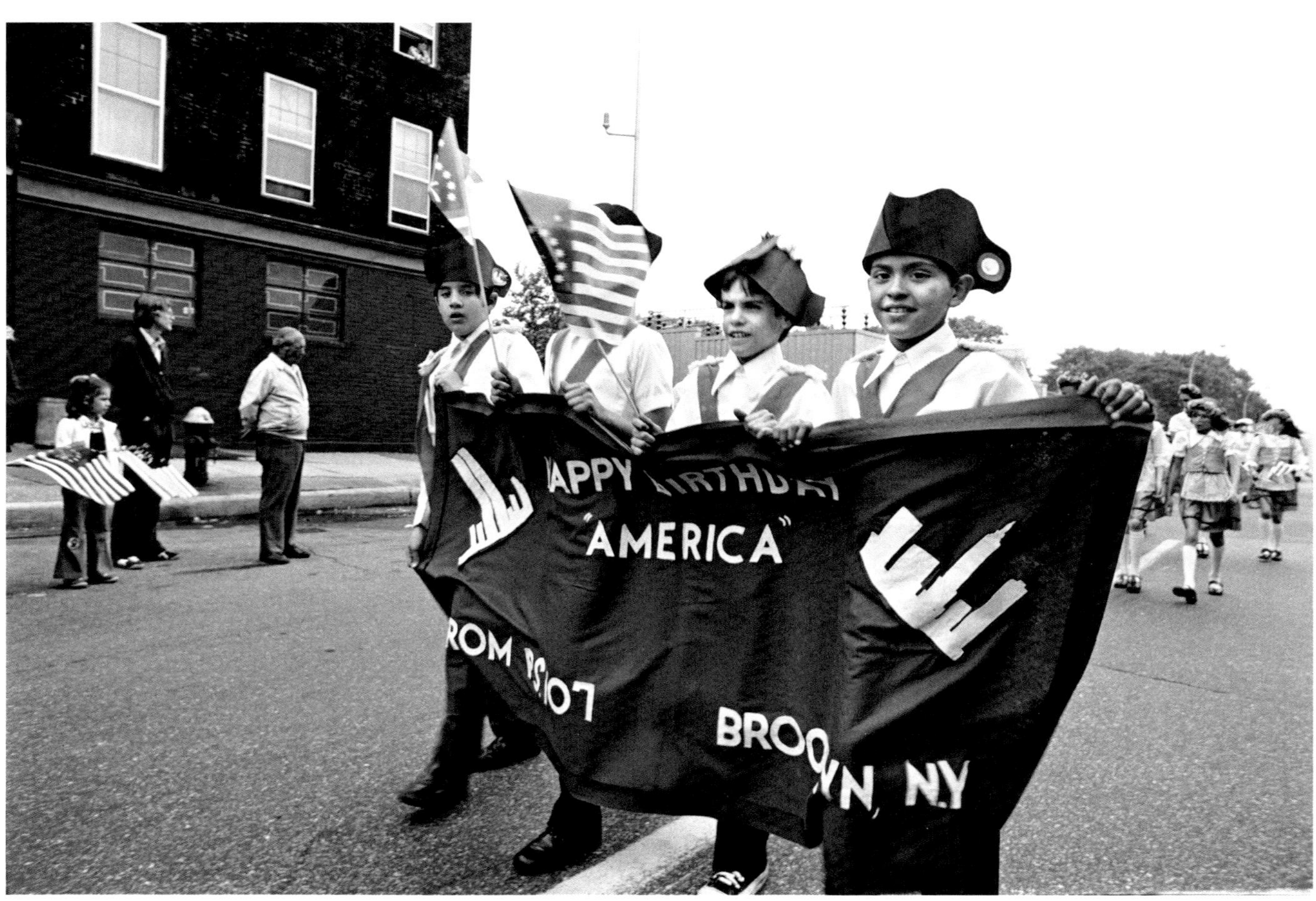

HAPPY BIRTHDAY
"AMERICA"
ROM PS107
LOYS
BROO'N, N.Y

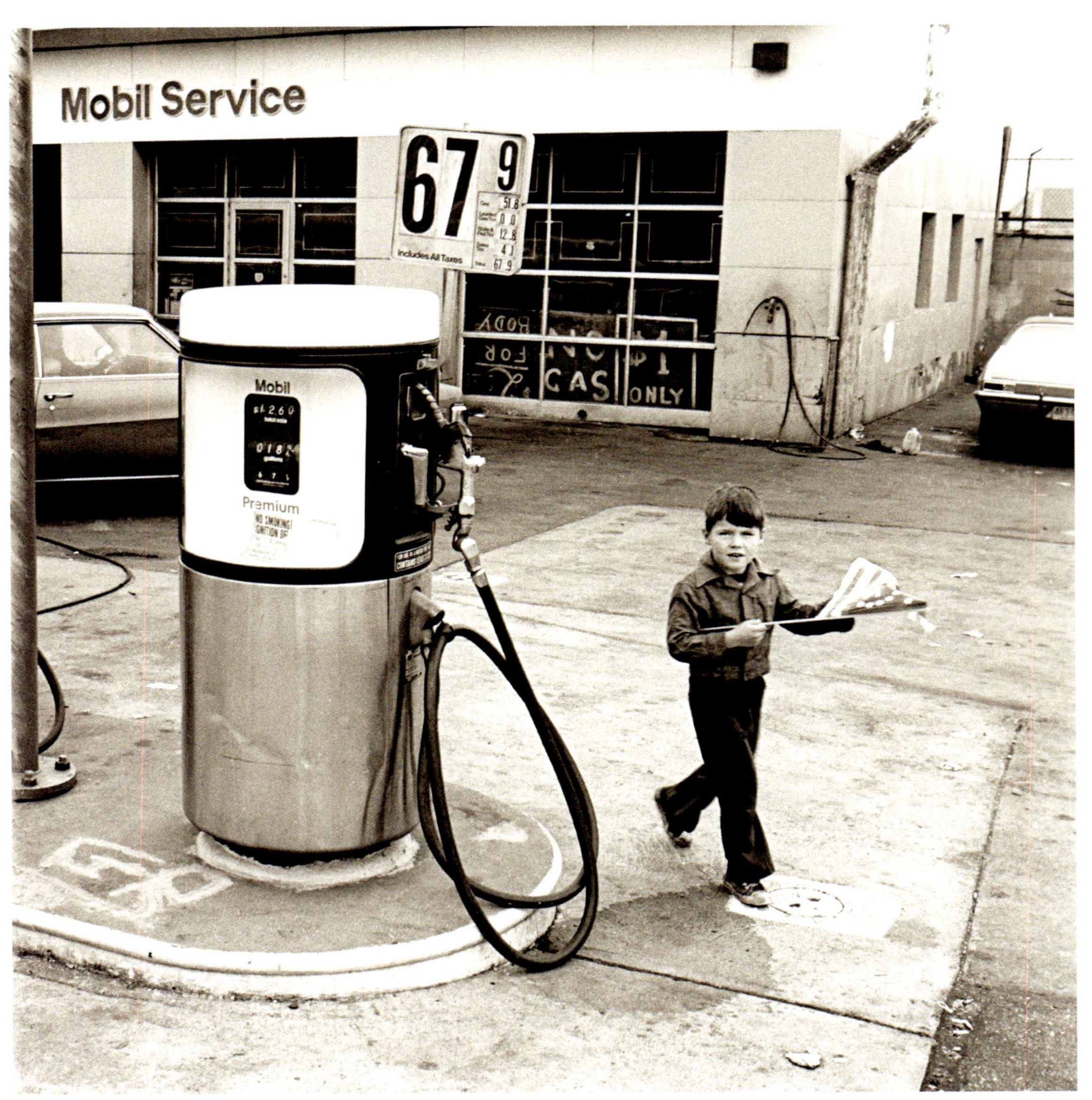

Mobil Service
67 9
Includes All Taxes
Mobil
Premium
NO SMOKING!
IGNITION OFF
GAS ONLY
BODY
FOR

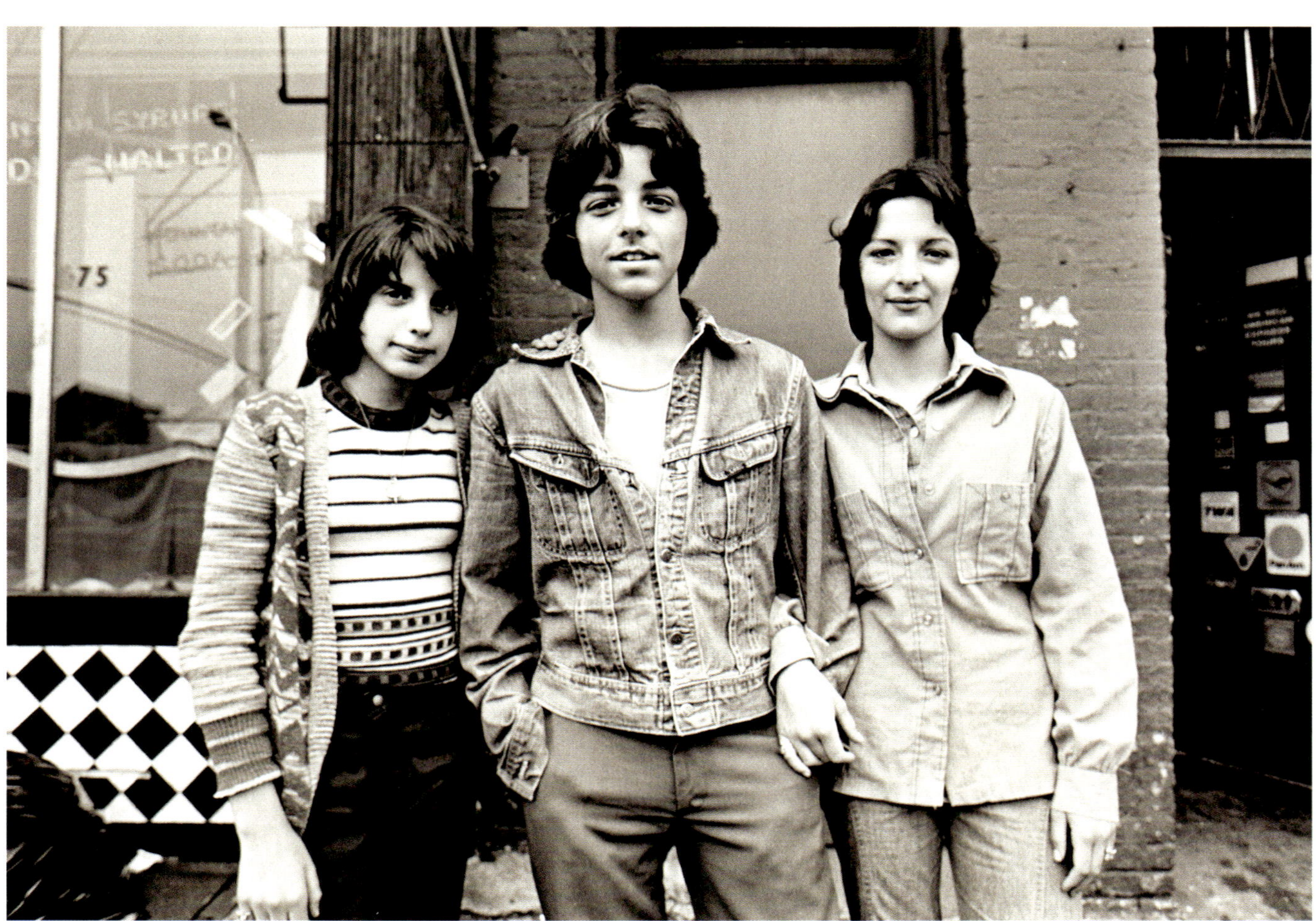

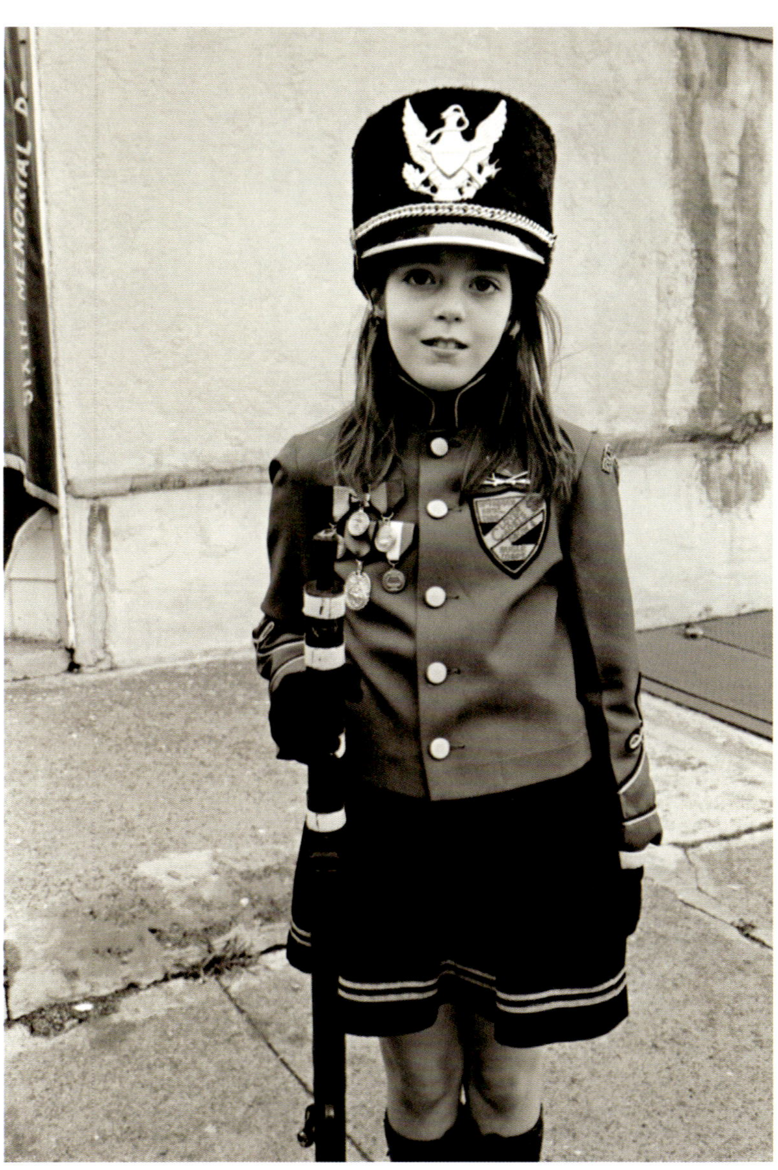

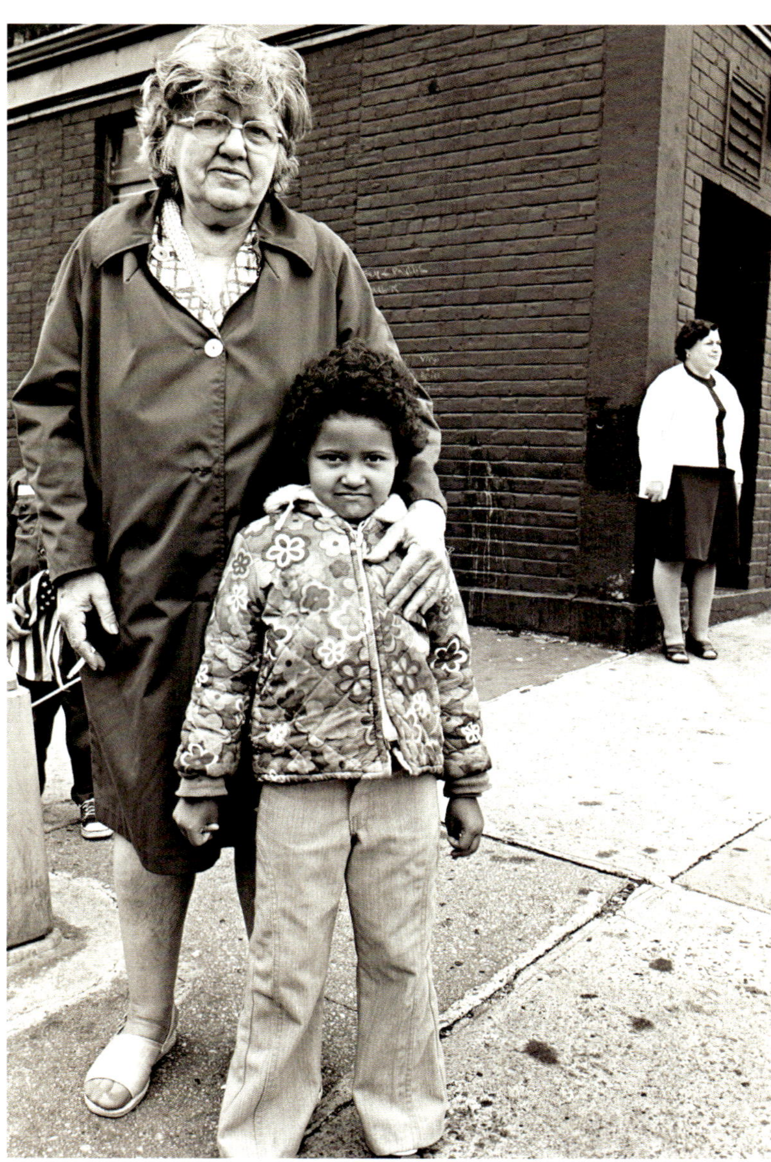

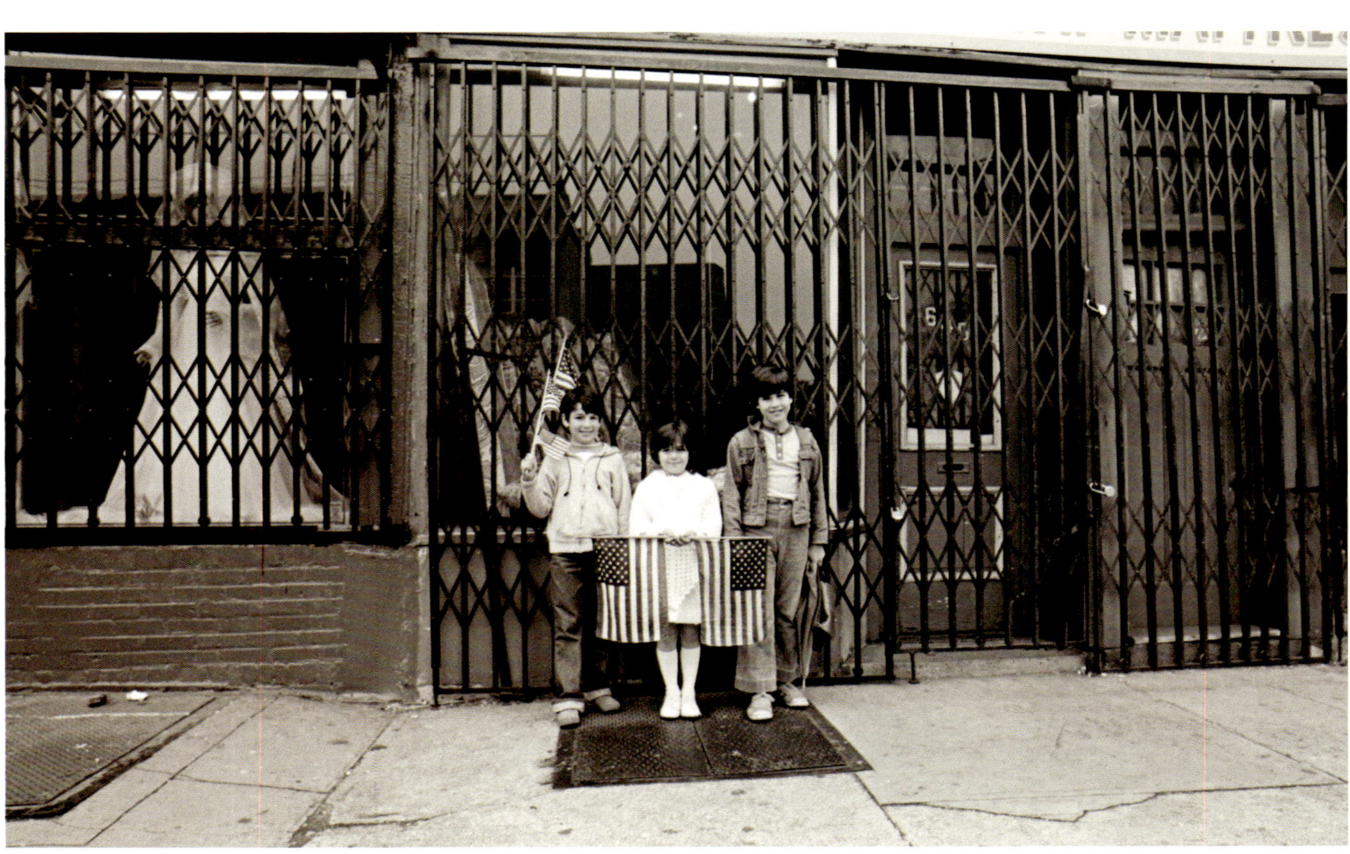

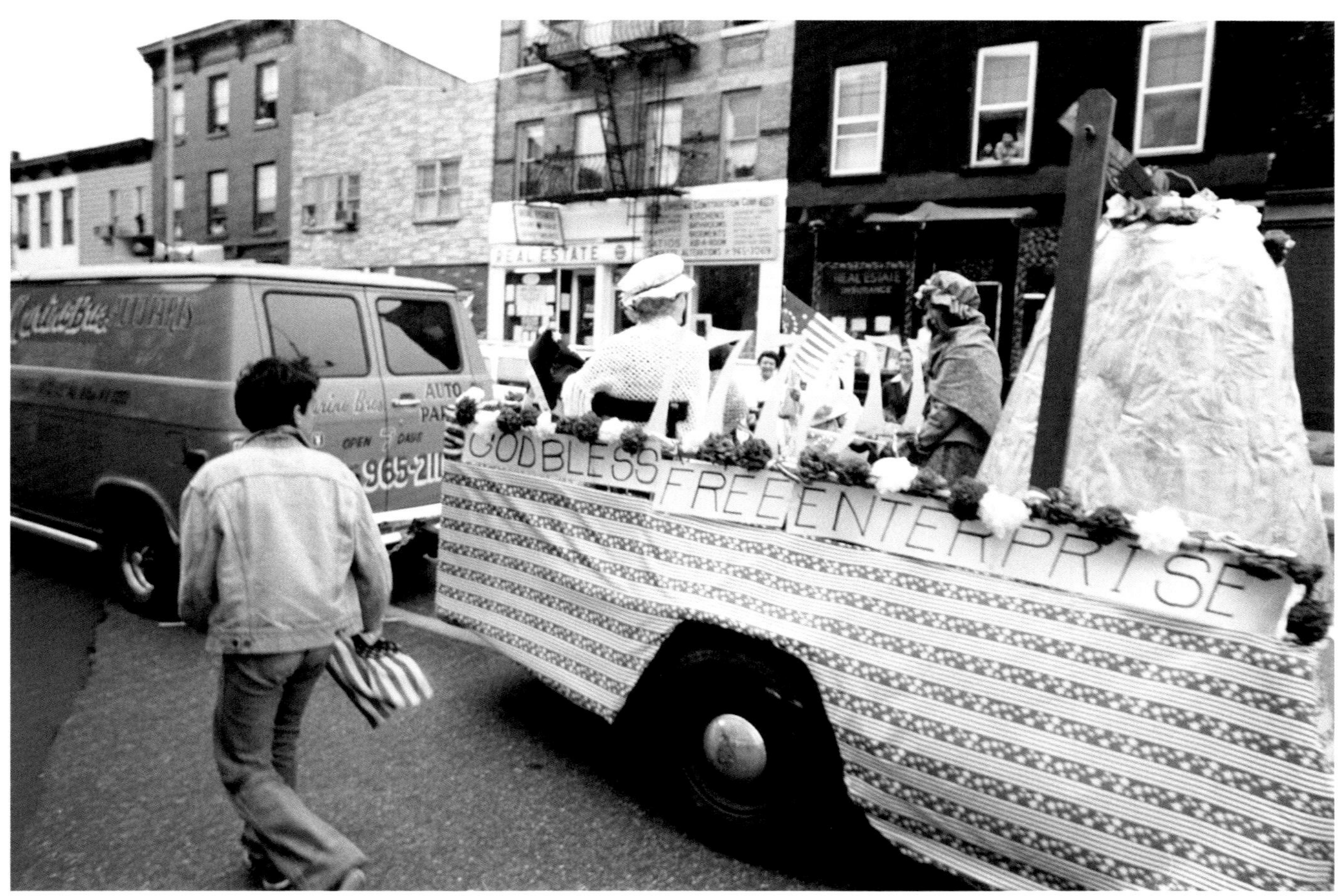
AUTO
PART
965-2110
REAL ESTATE
REAL ESTATE
INSURANCE
GOD BLESS FREE ENTERPRISE

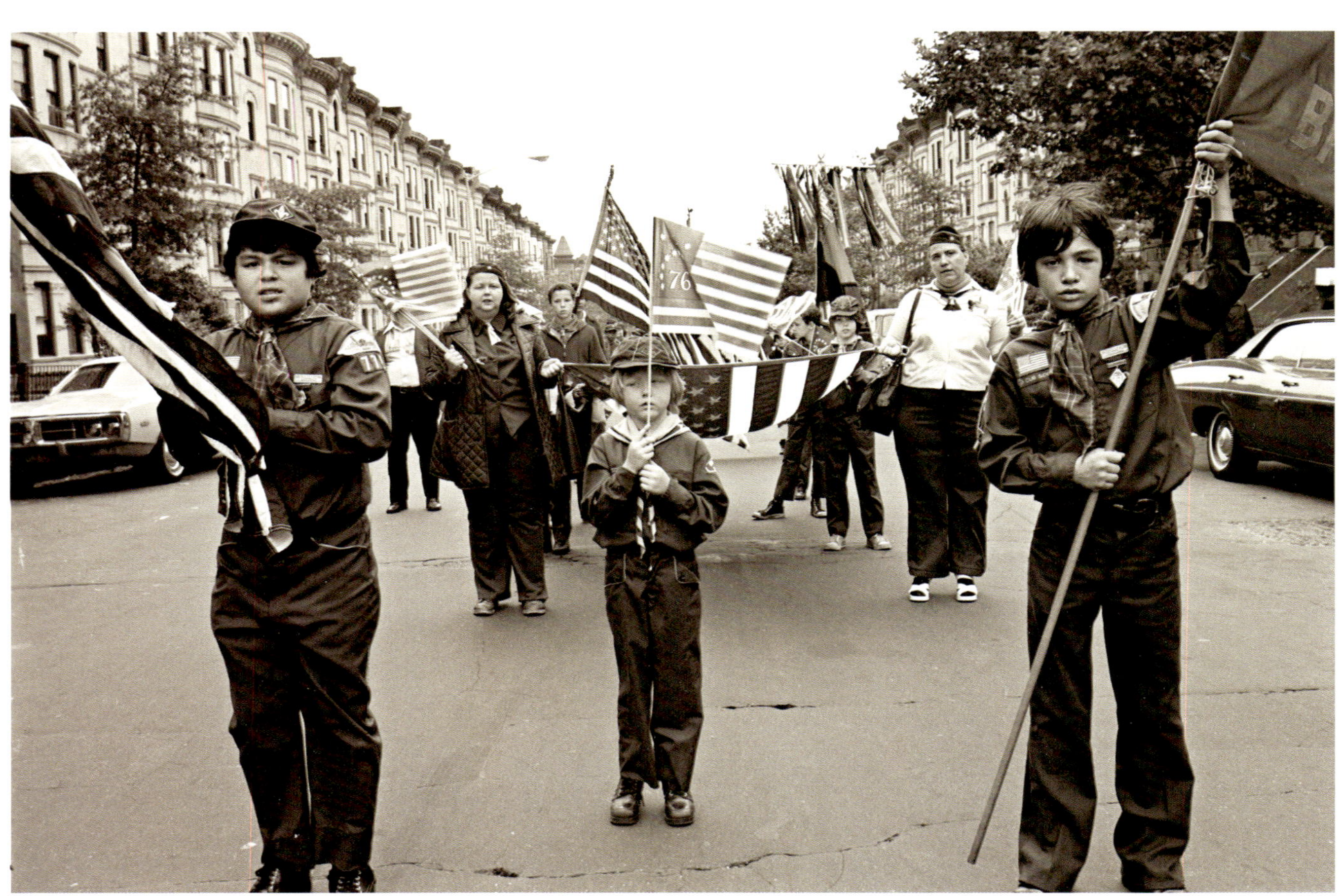

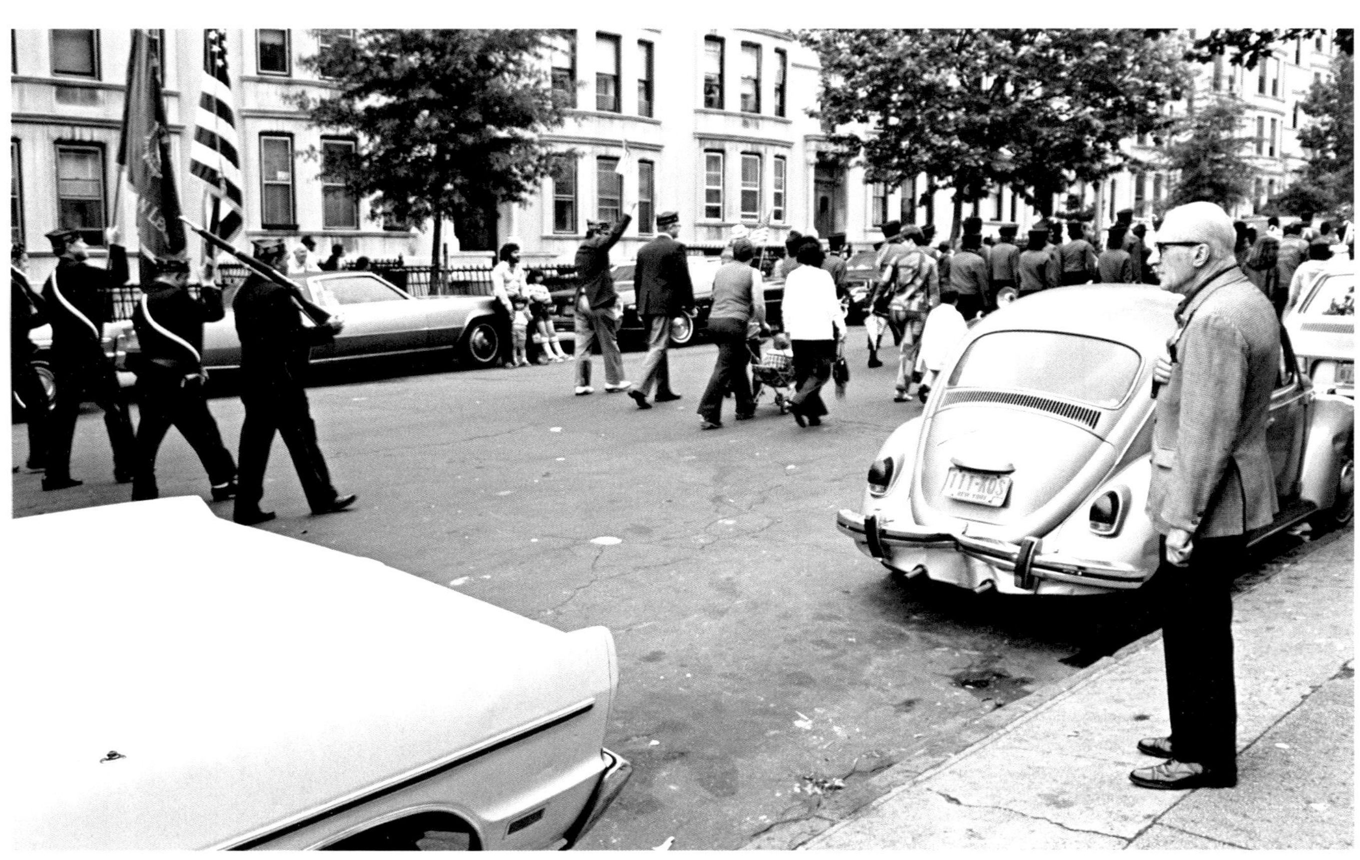

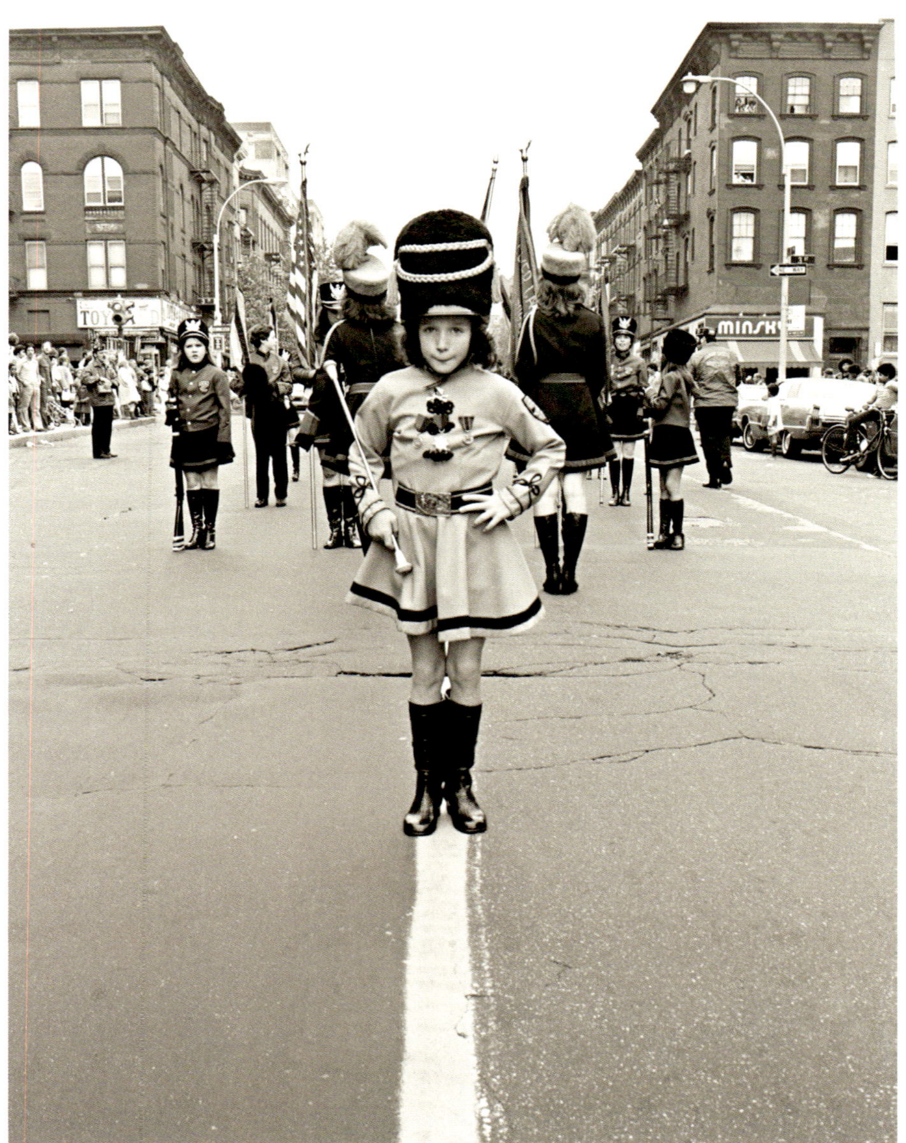

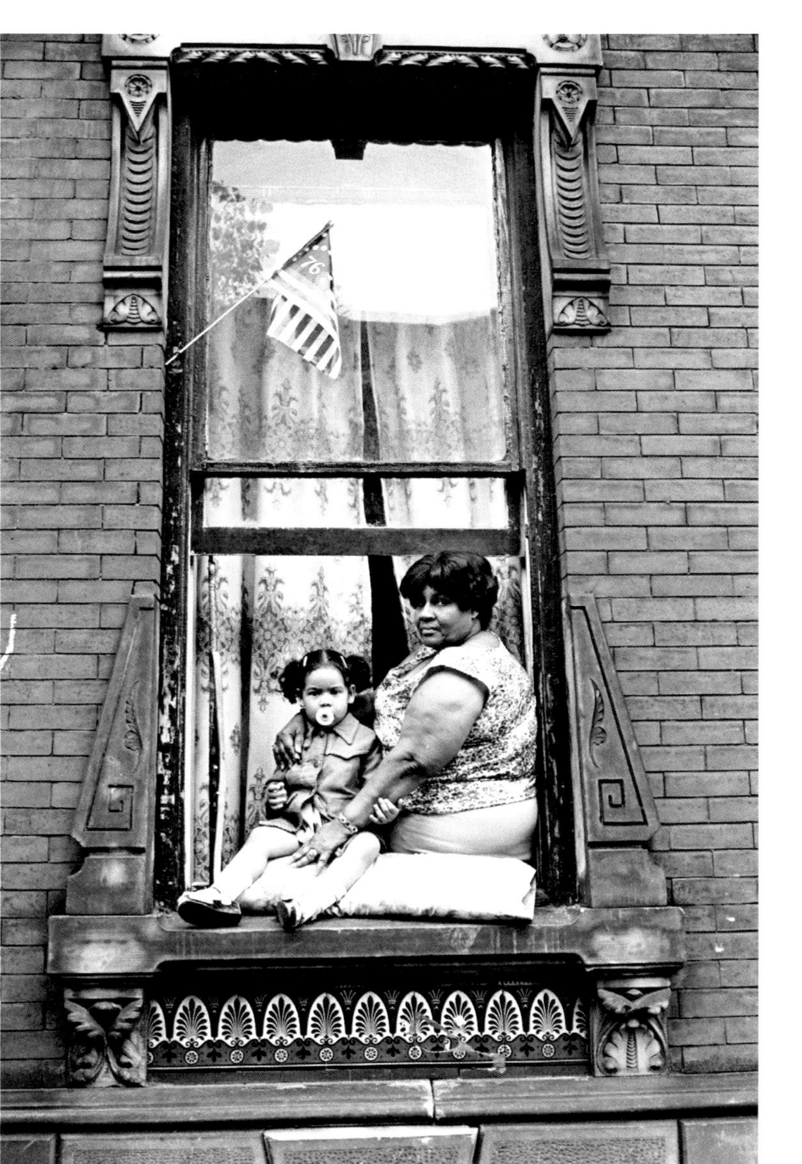

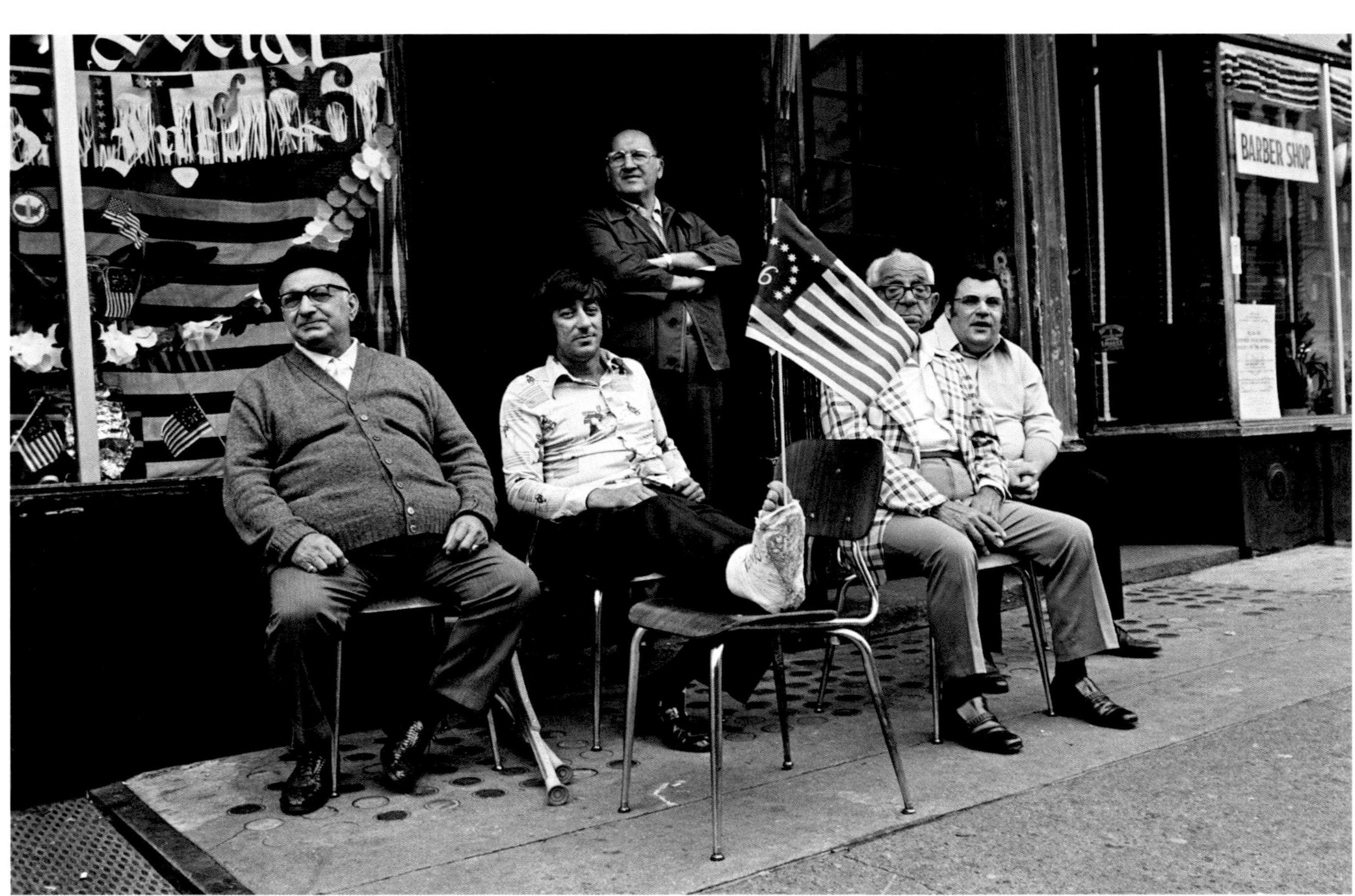
BARBER SHOP

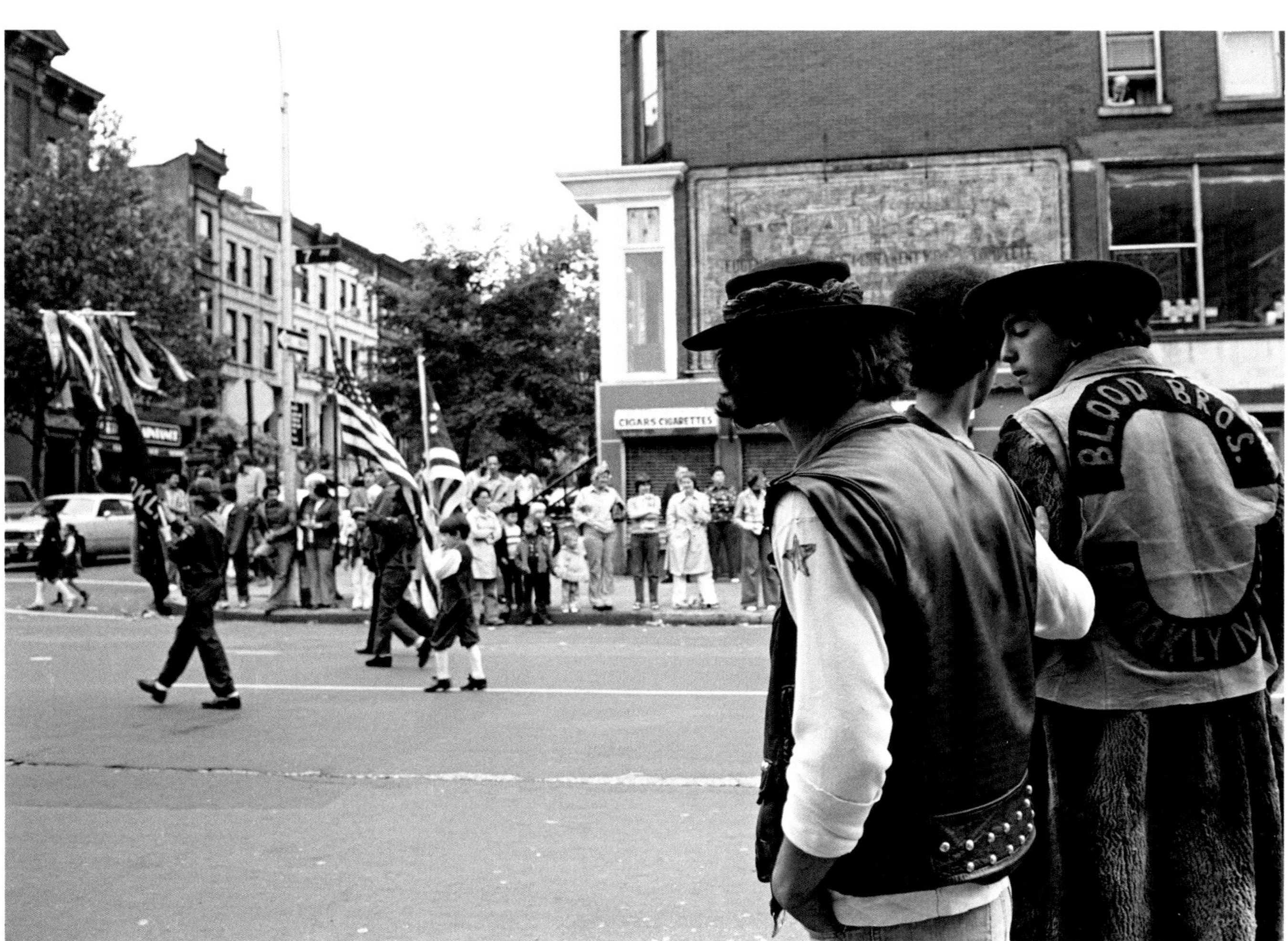

BLOOD BROS.
BROOKLYN
CIGARS CIGARETTES

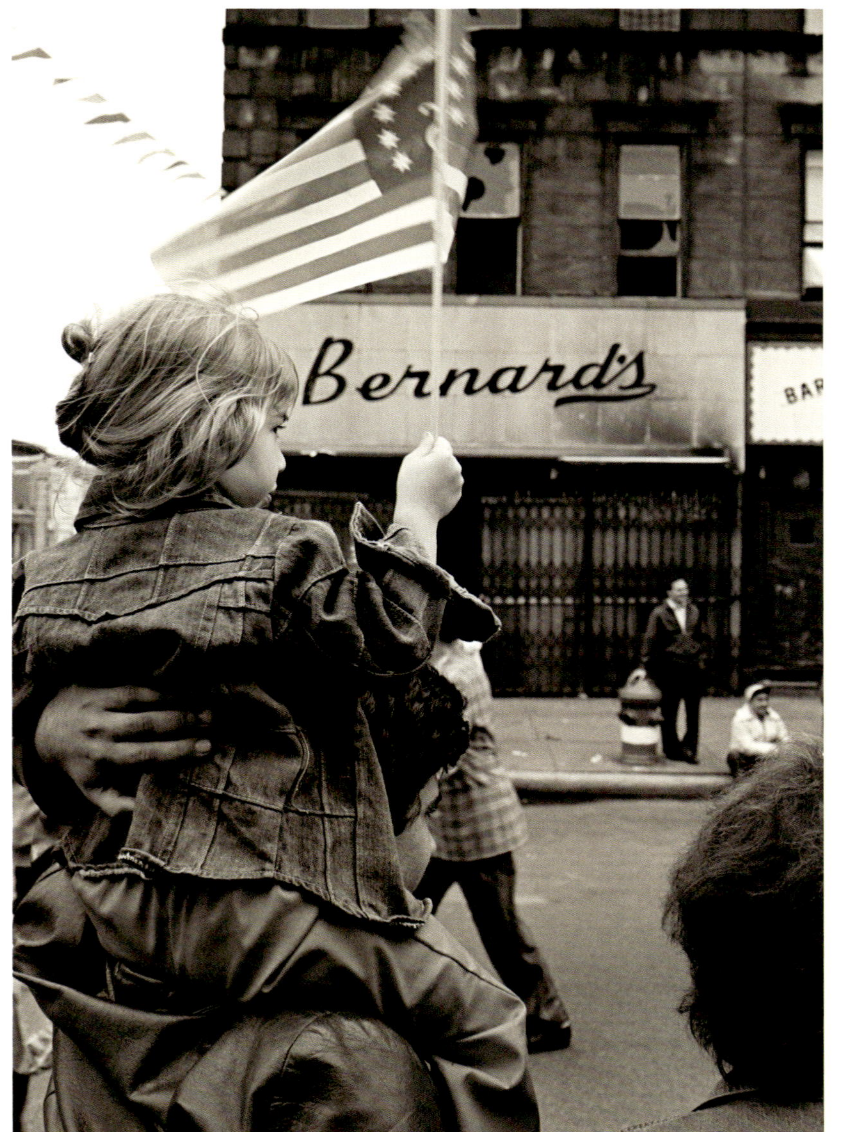
Bernard's
BAR

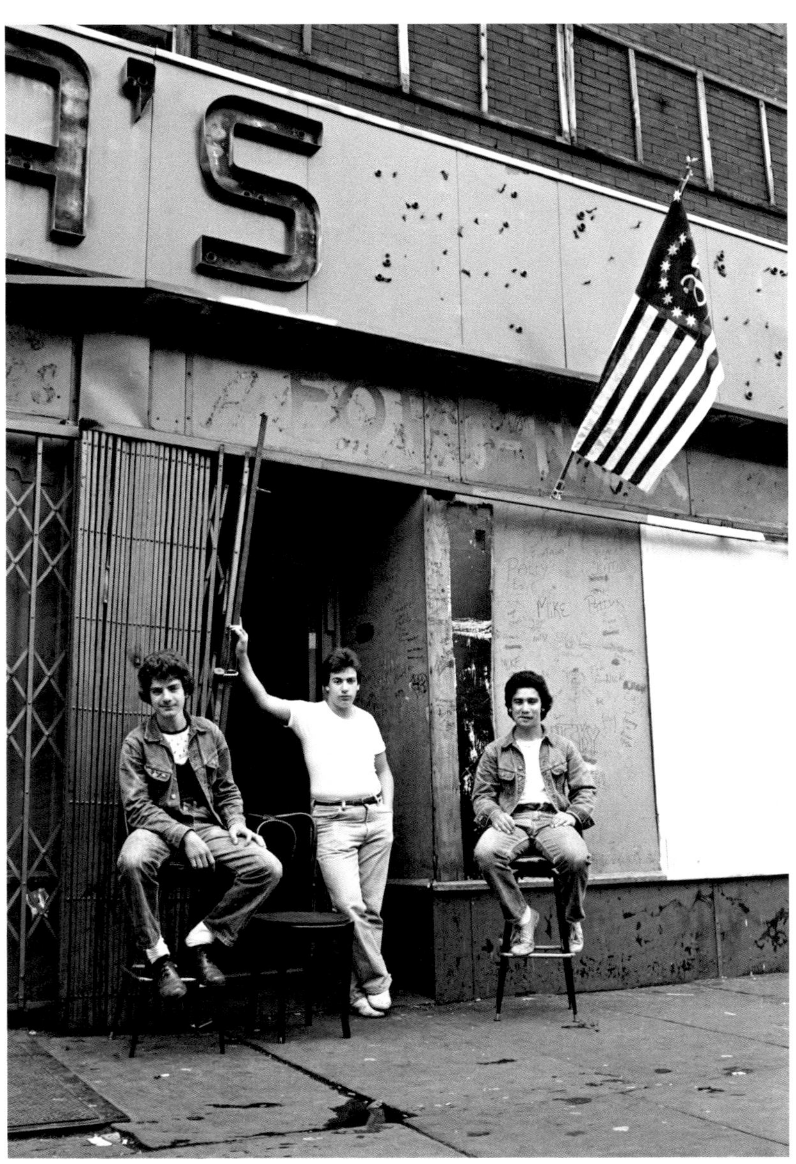

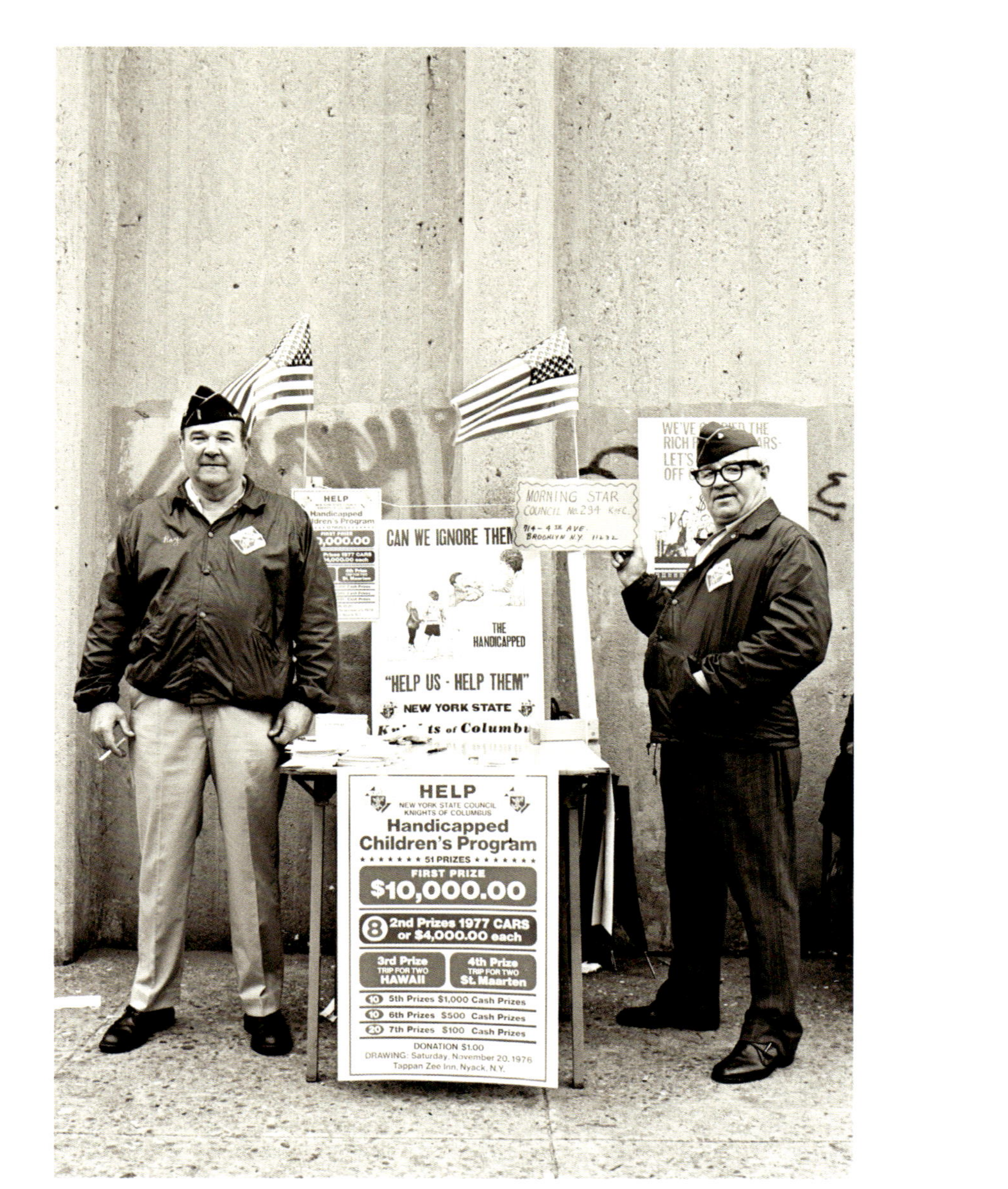
MORNING STAR
COUNCIL No.234 K of C.
914 - 4 th AVE
BROOKLYN N.Y. 11232

CAN WE IGNORE THEM
THE
HANDICAPPED
"HELP US - HELP THEM"
NEW YORK STATE
Knights of Columbus

HELP
NEW YORK STATE COUNCIL
KNIGHTS OF COLUMBUS
Handicapped
Children's Program
51 PRIZES
FIRST PRIZE
$10,000.00
8 2nd Prizes 1977 CARS
or $4,000.00 each
3rd Prize
TRIP FOR TWO
HAWAII
4th Prize
TRIP FOR TWO
St. Maarten
10 5th Prizes $1,000 Cash Prizes
10 6th Prizes $500 Cash Prizes
20 7th Prizes $100 Cash Prizes
DONATION $1.00
DRAWING: Saturday, November 20, 1976
Tappan Zee Inn, Nyack, N.Y.

HELP
Handicapped
Children's Program

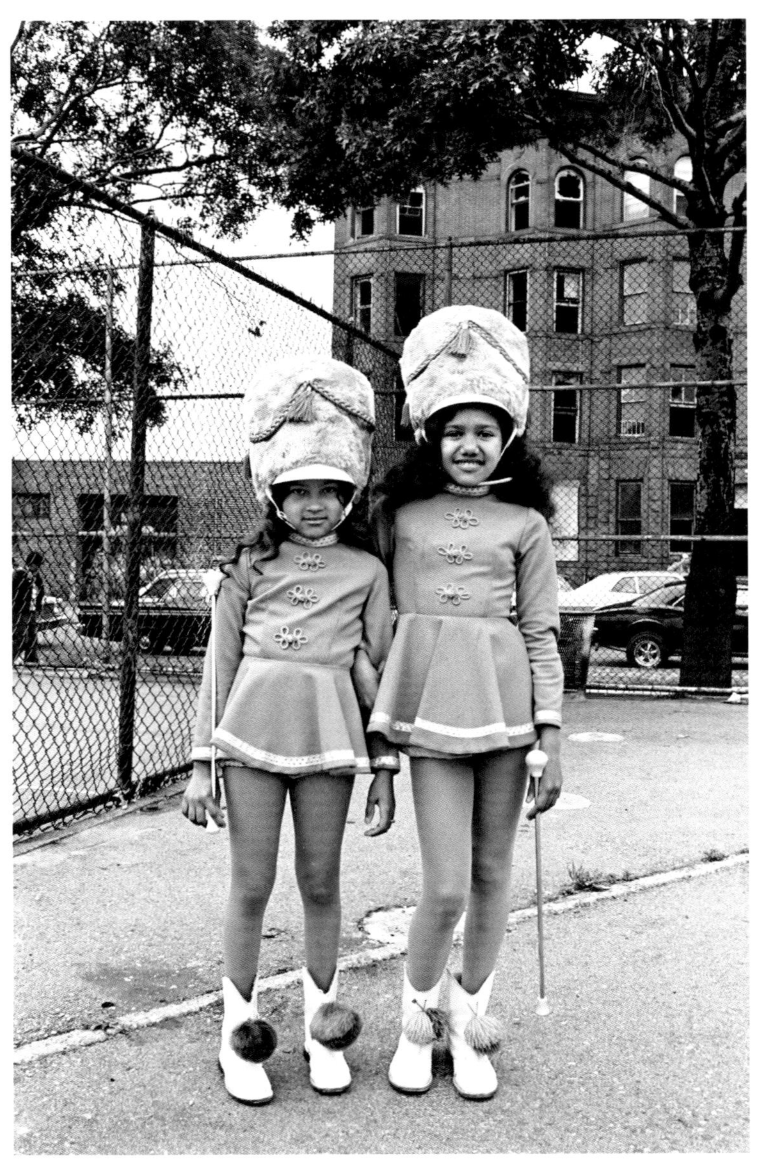

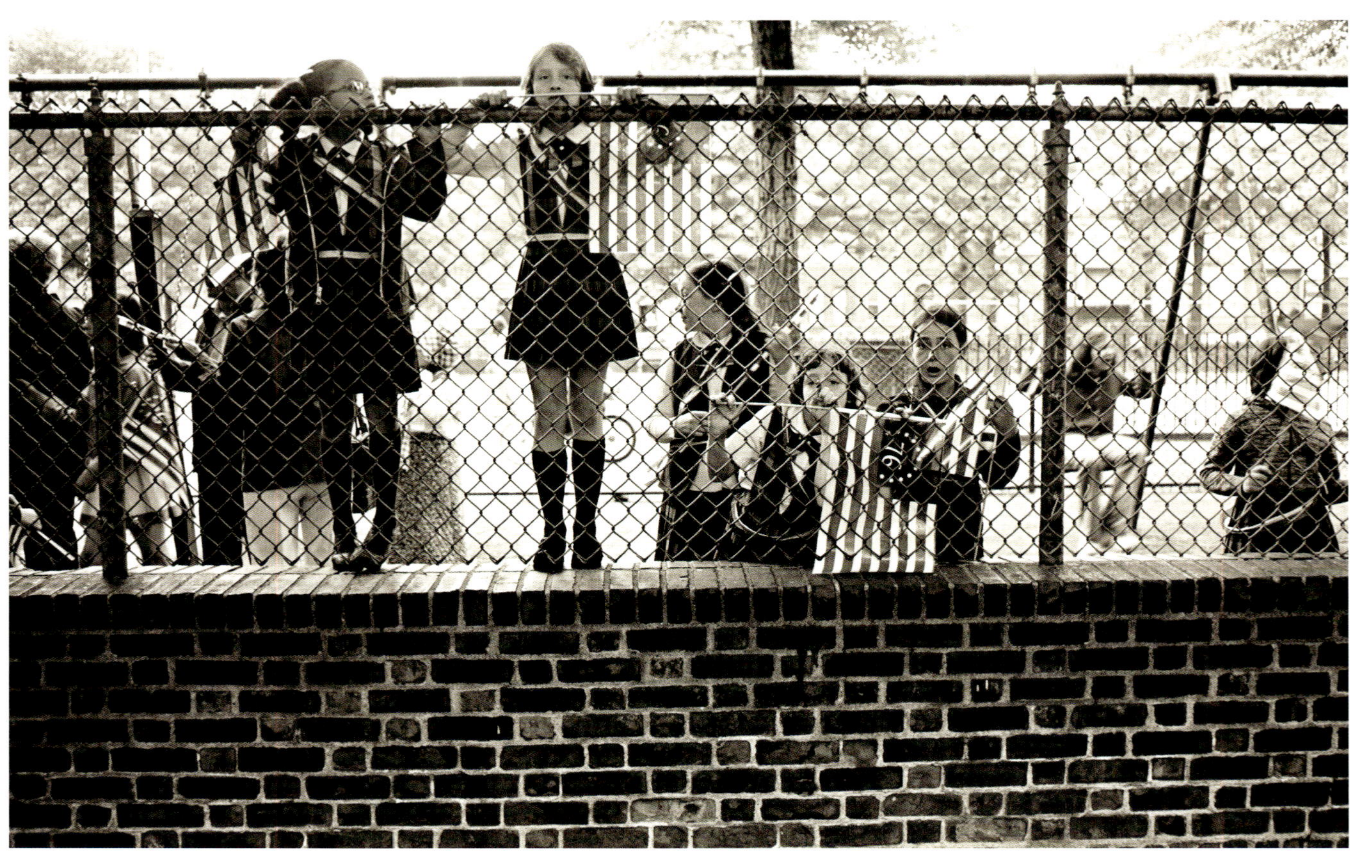

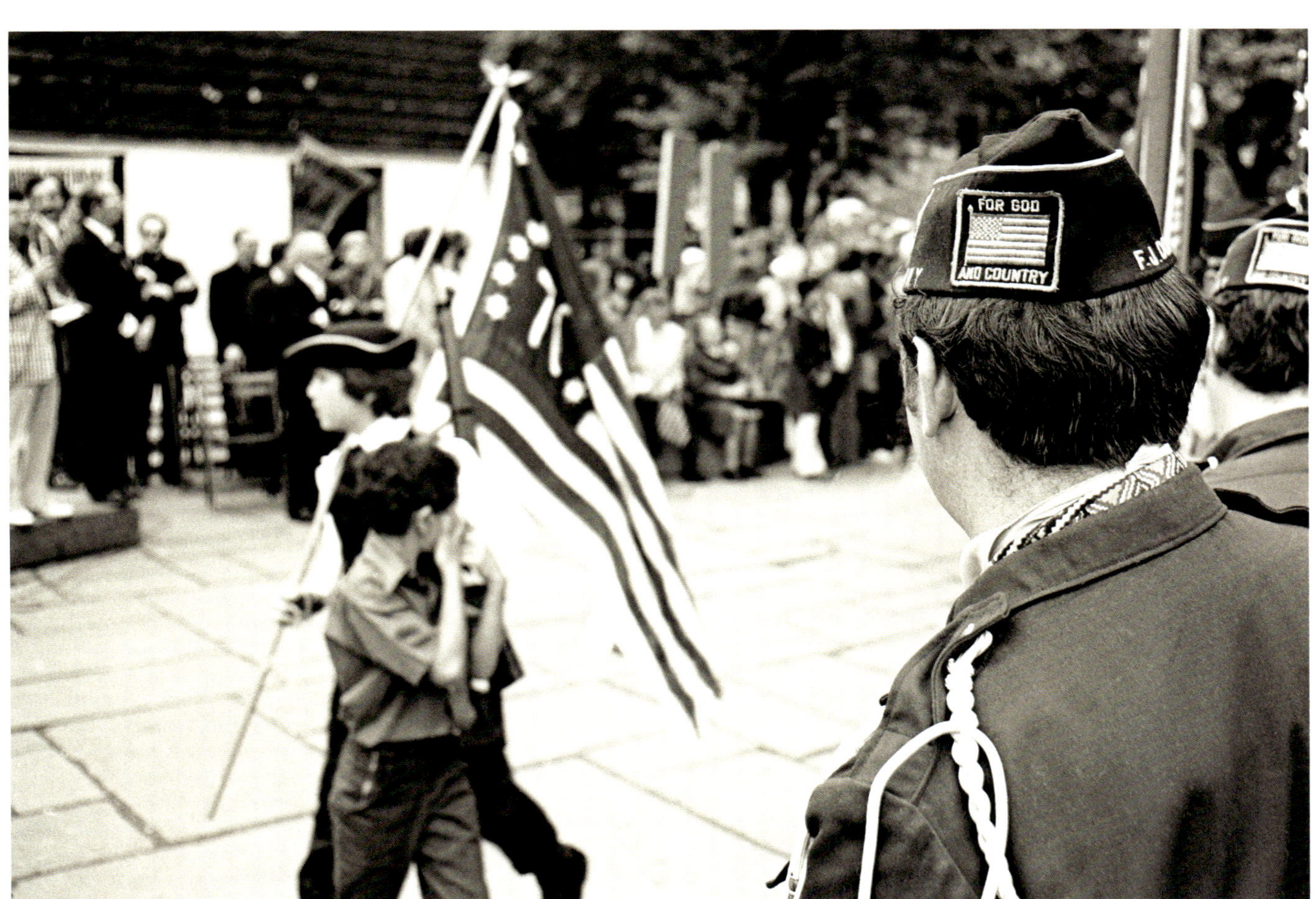

FOR GOD
AND COUNTRY

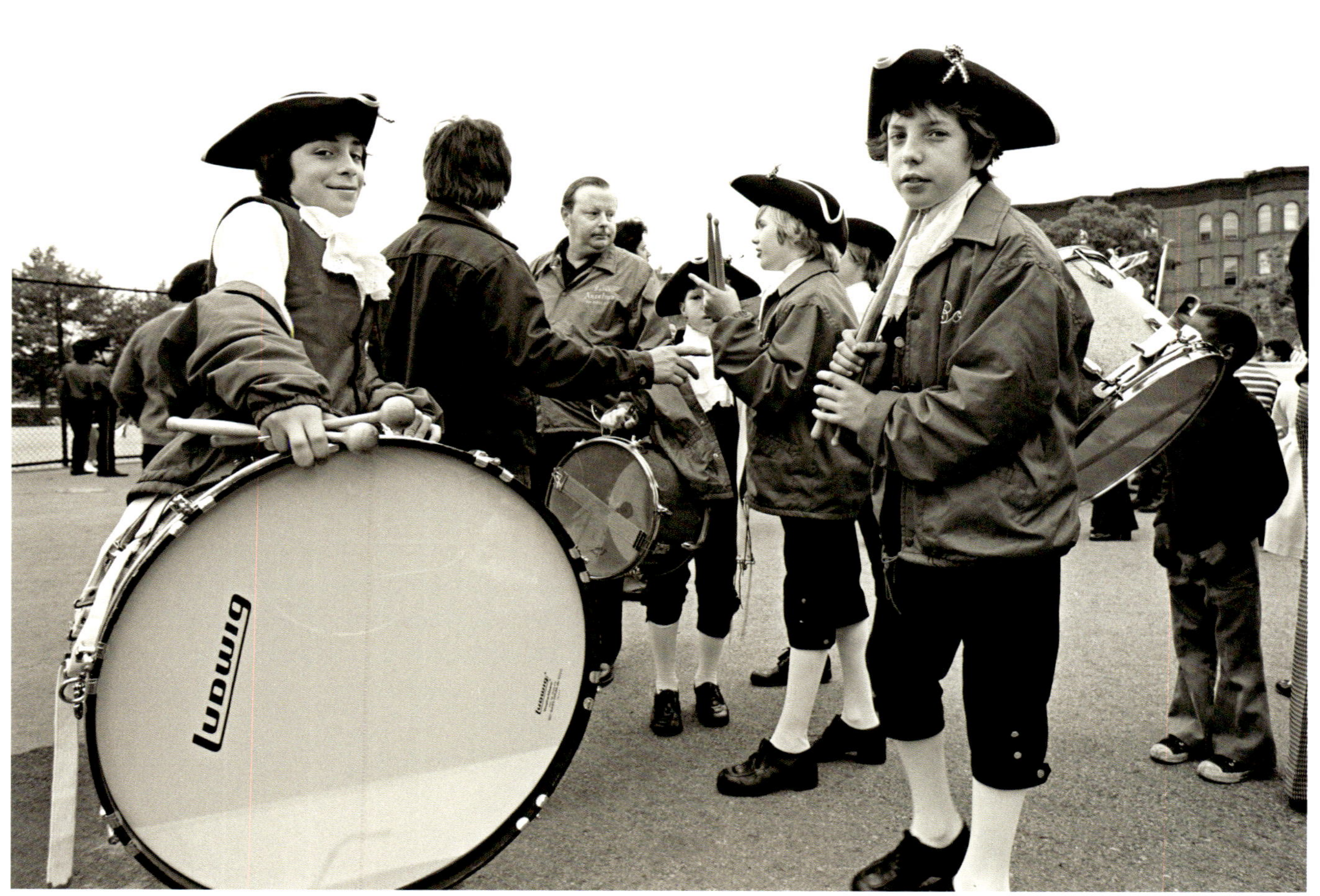

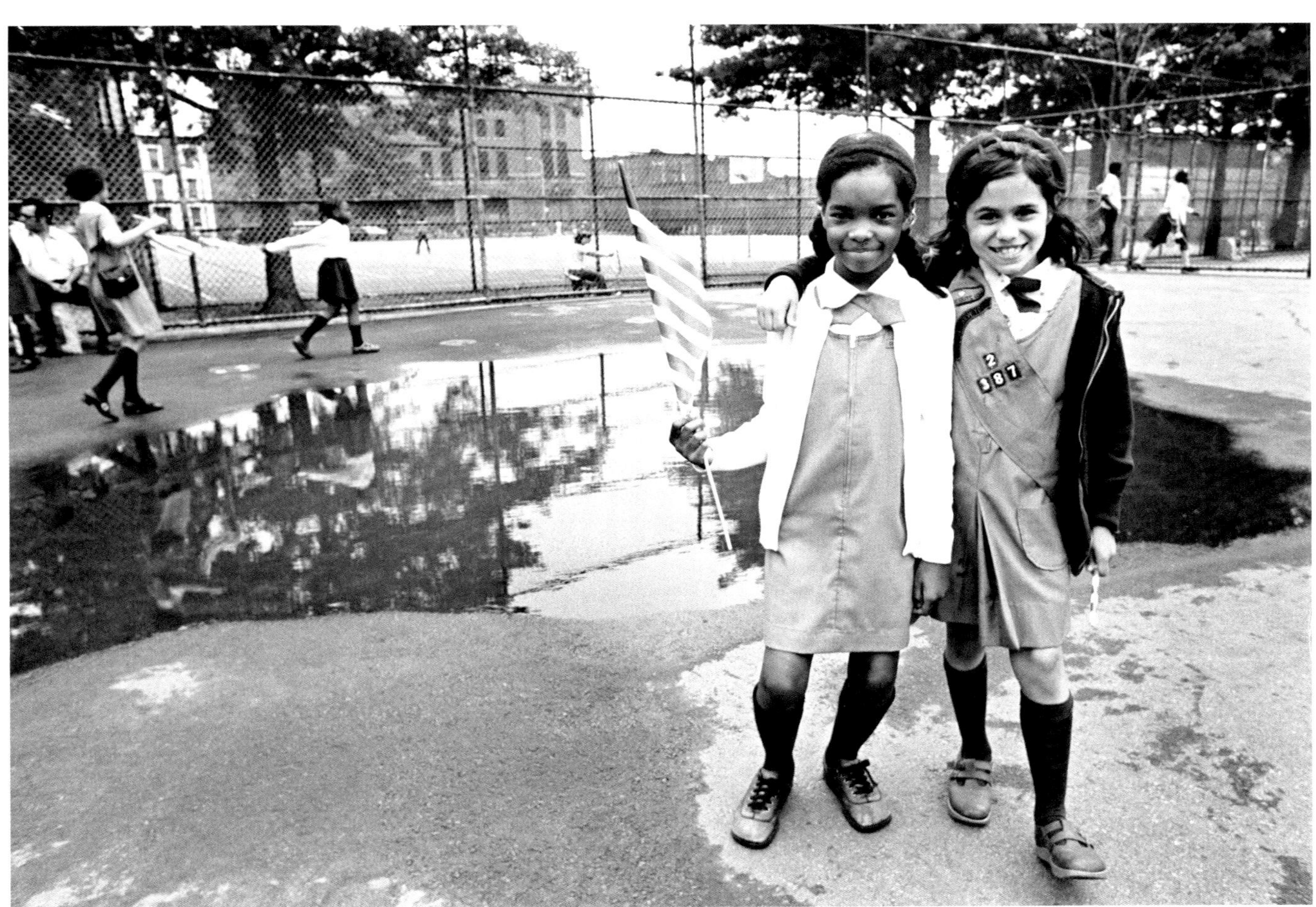

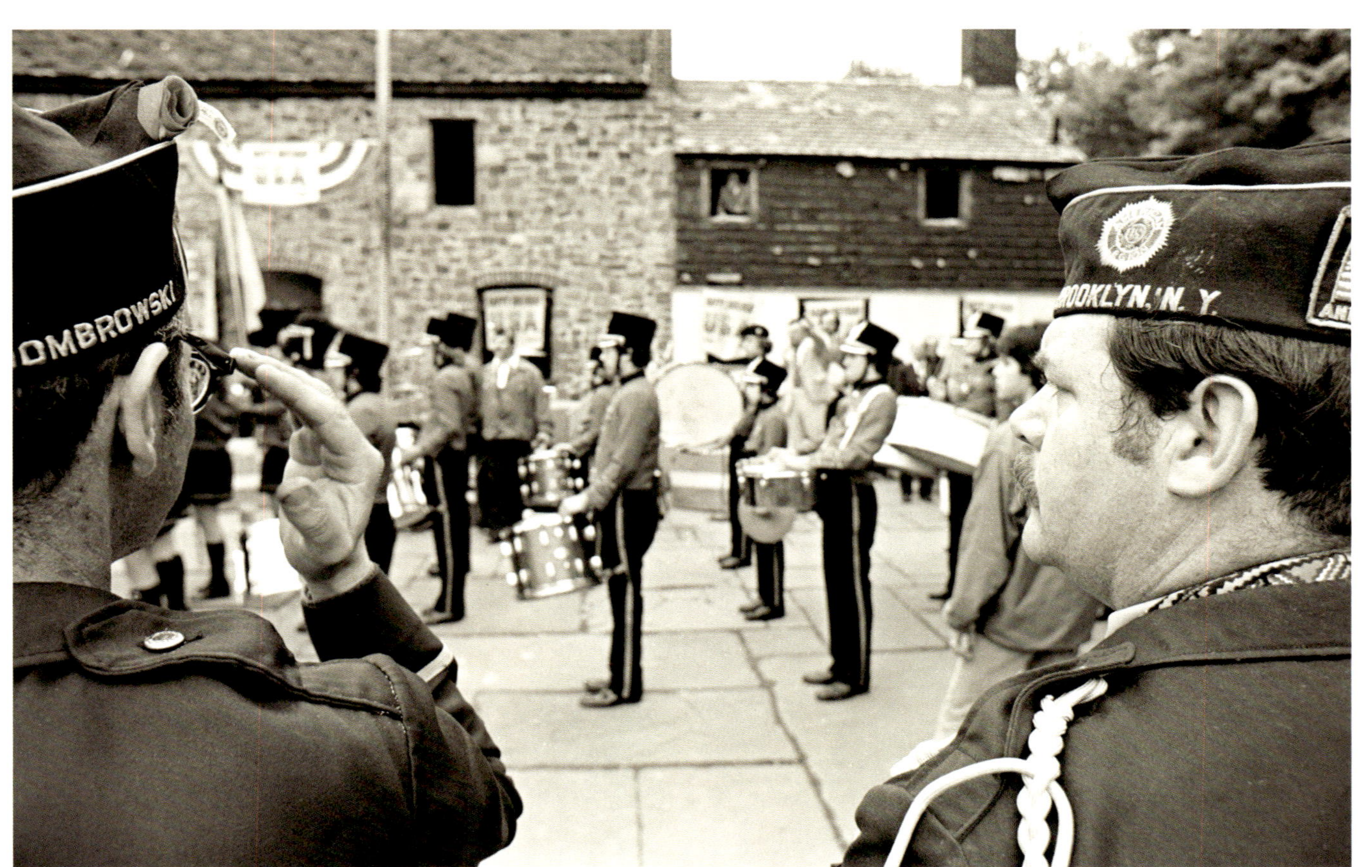
OMBROWSKI
BROOKLYN, N.Y.

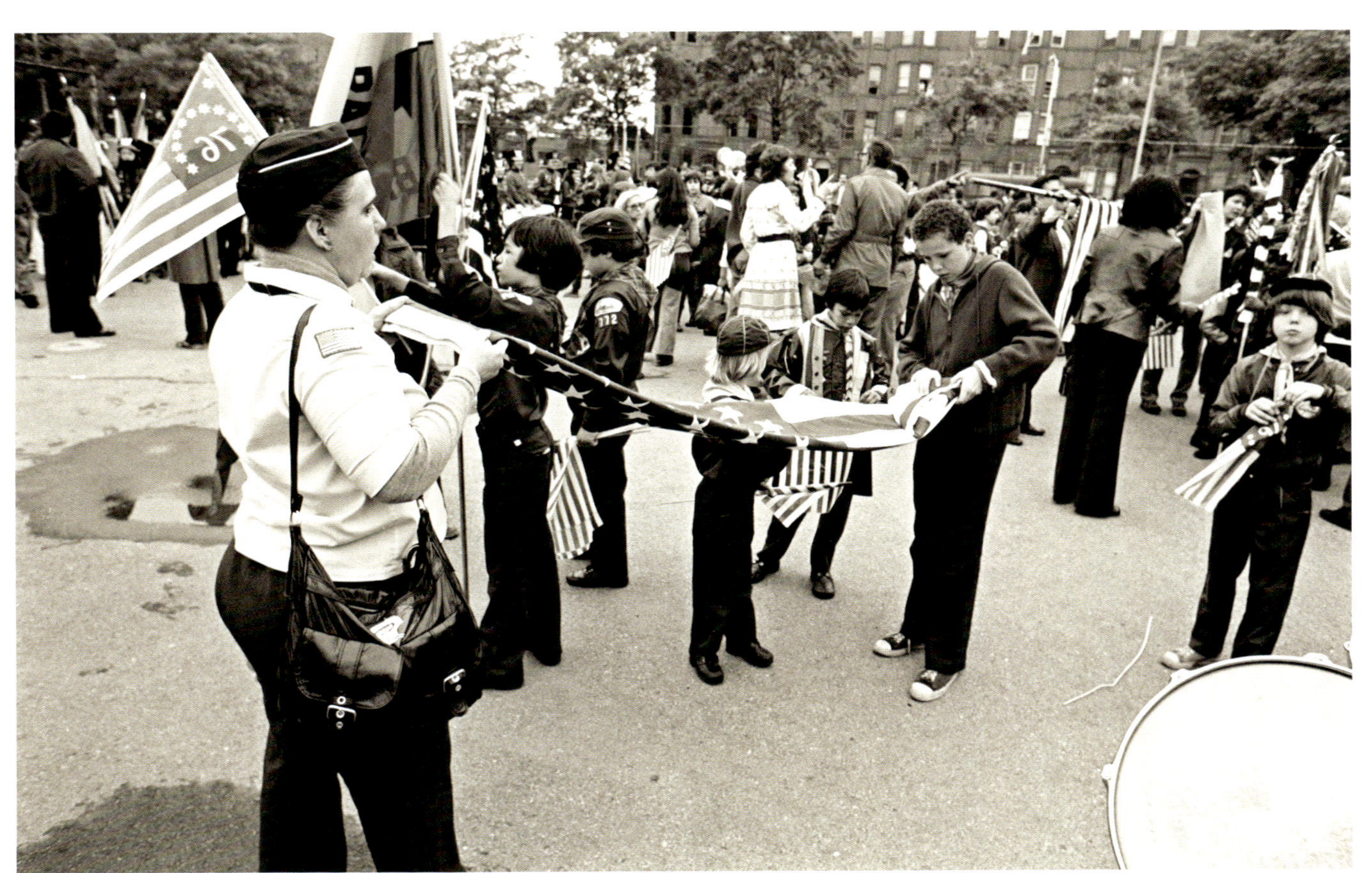

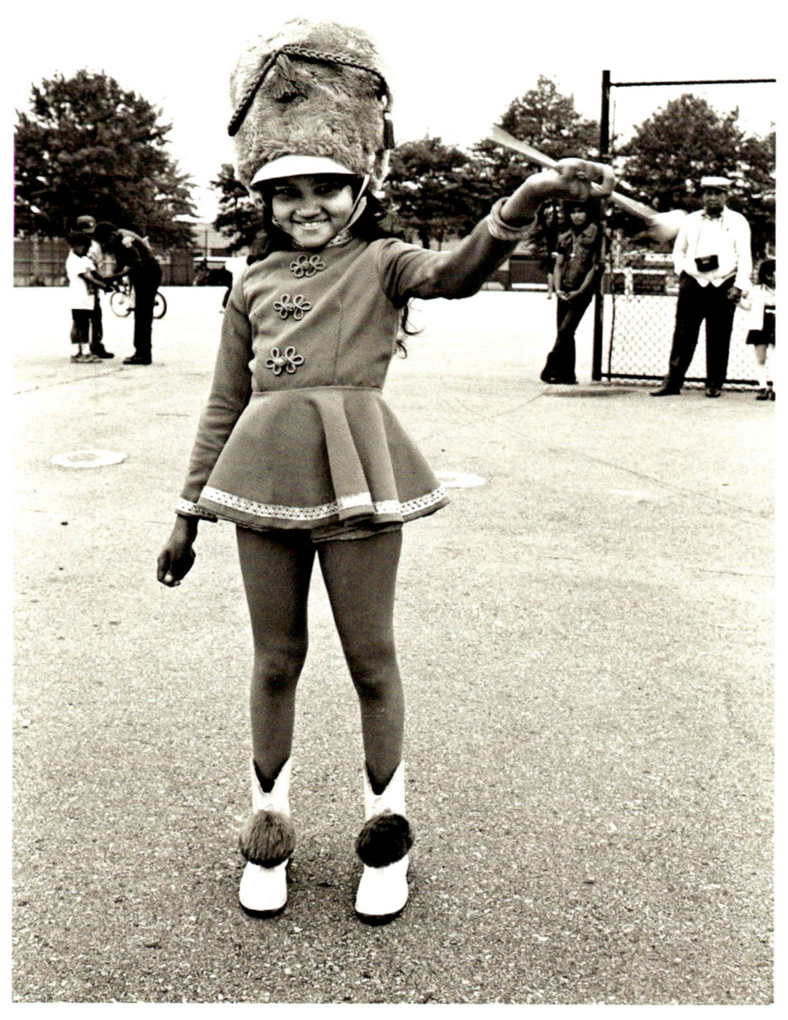

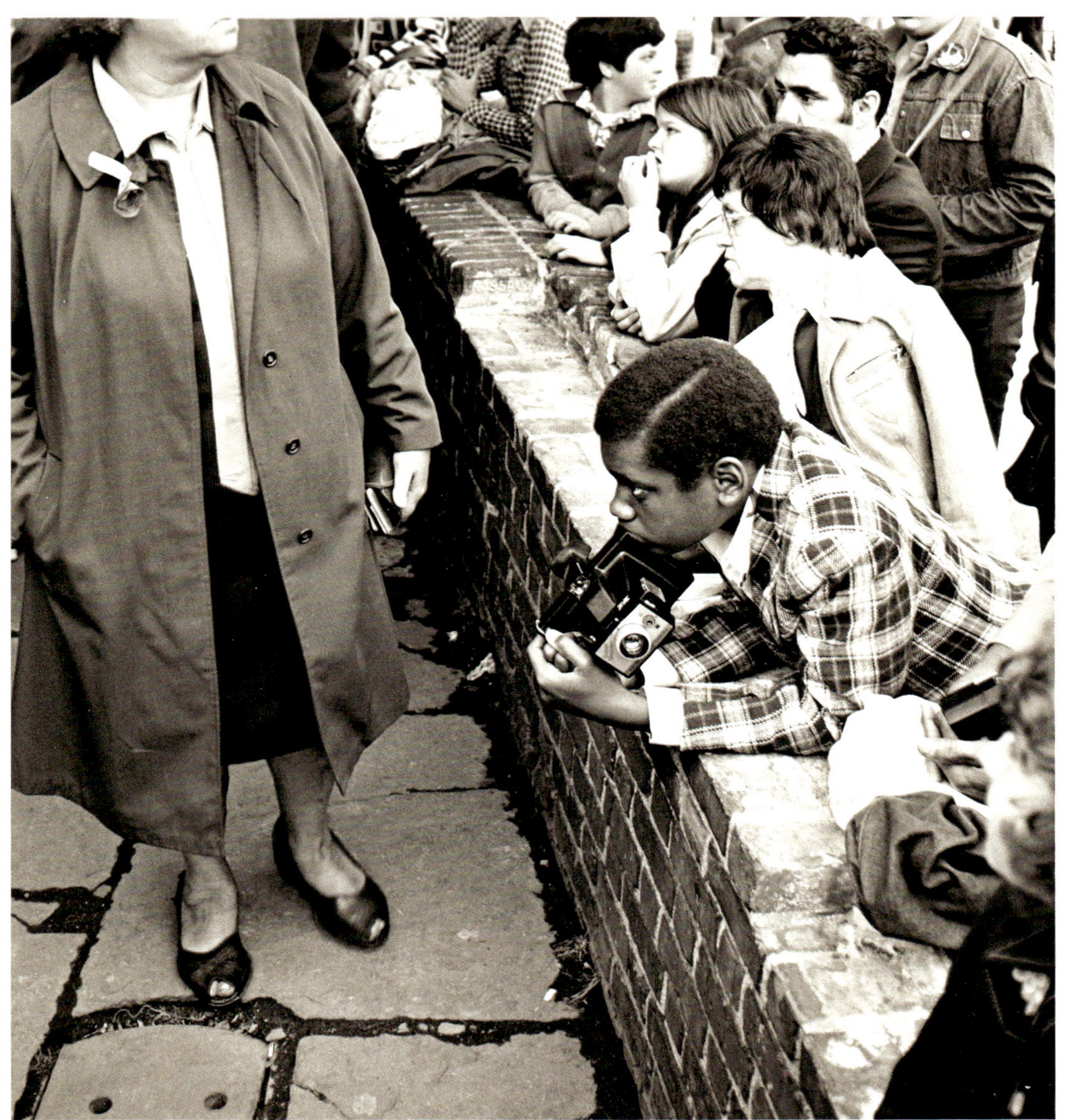

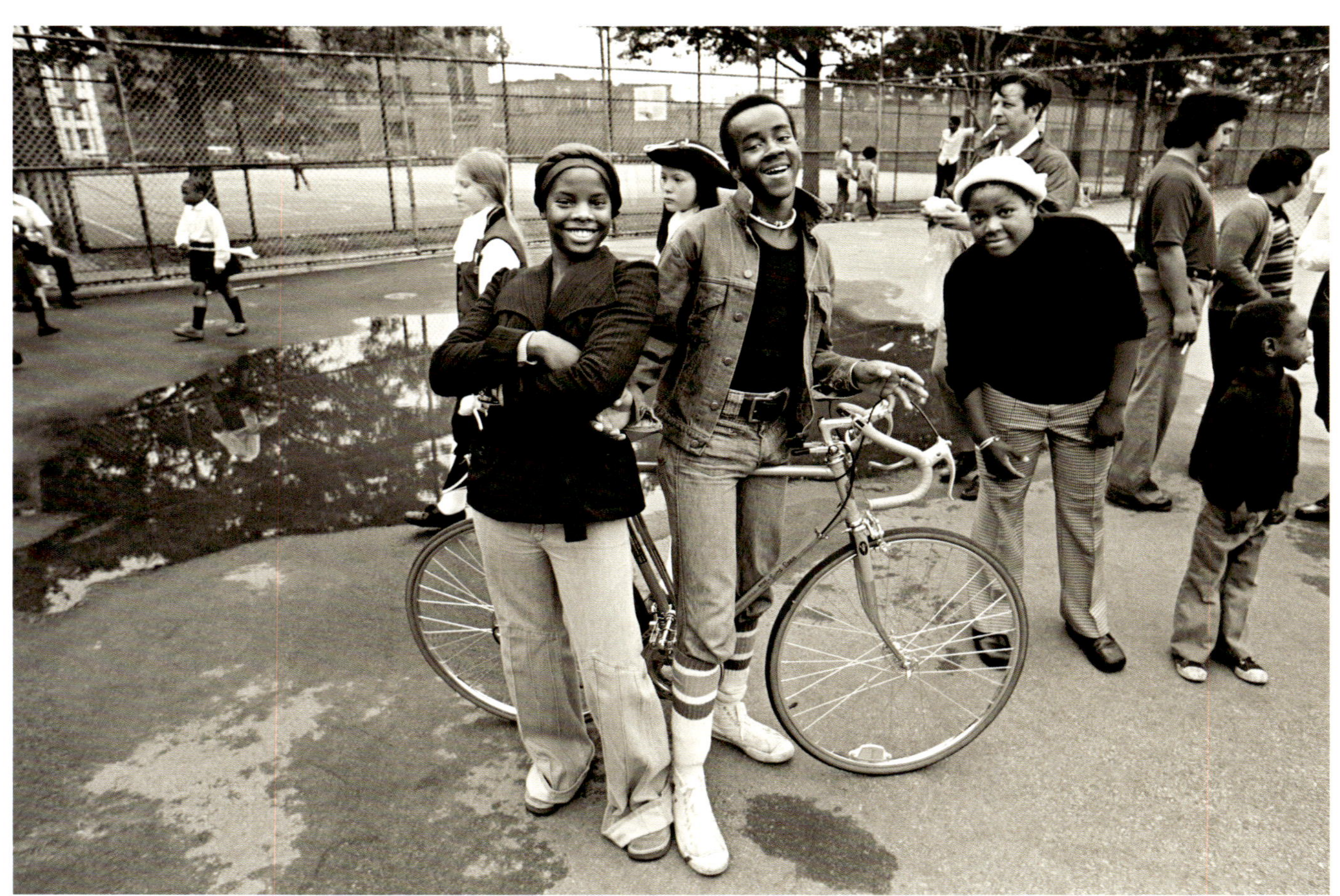

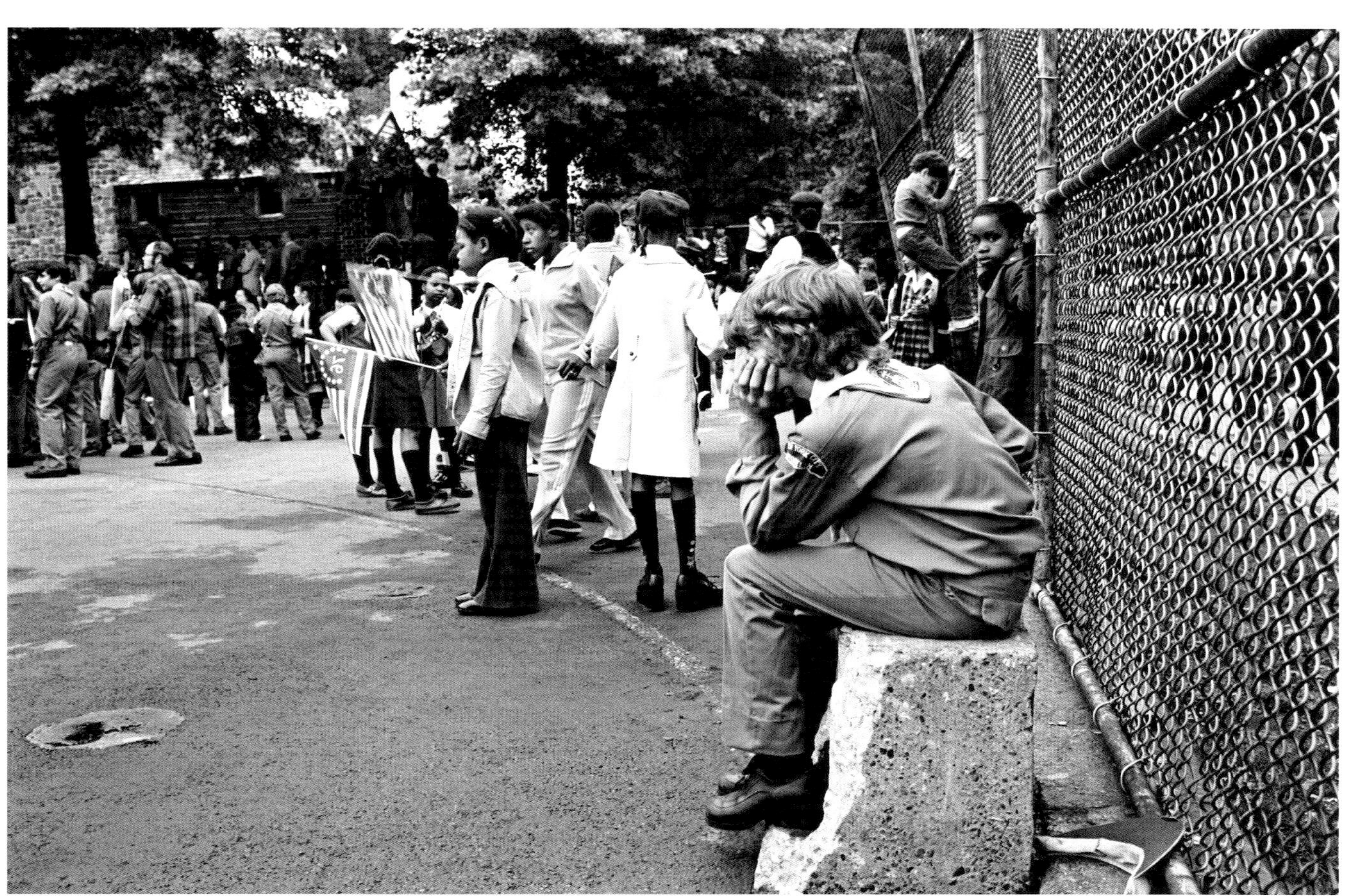

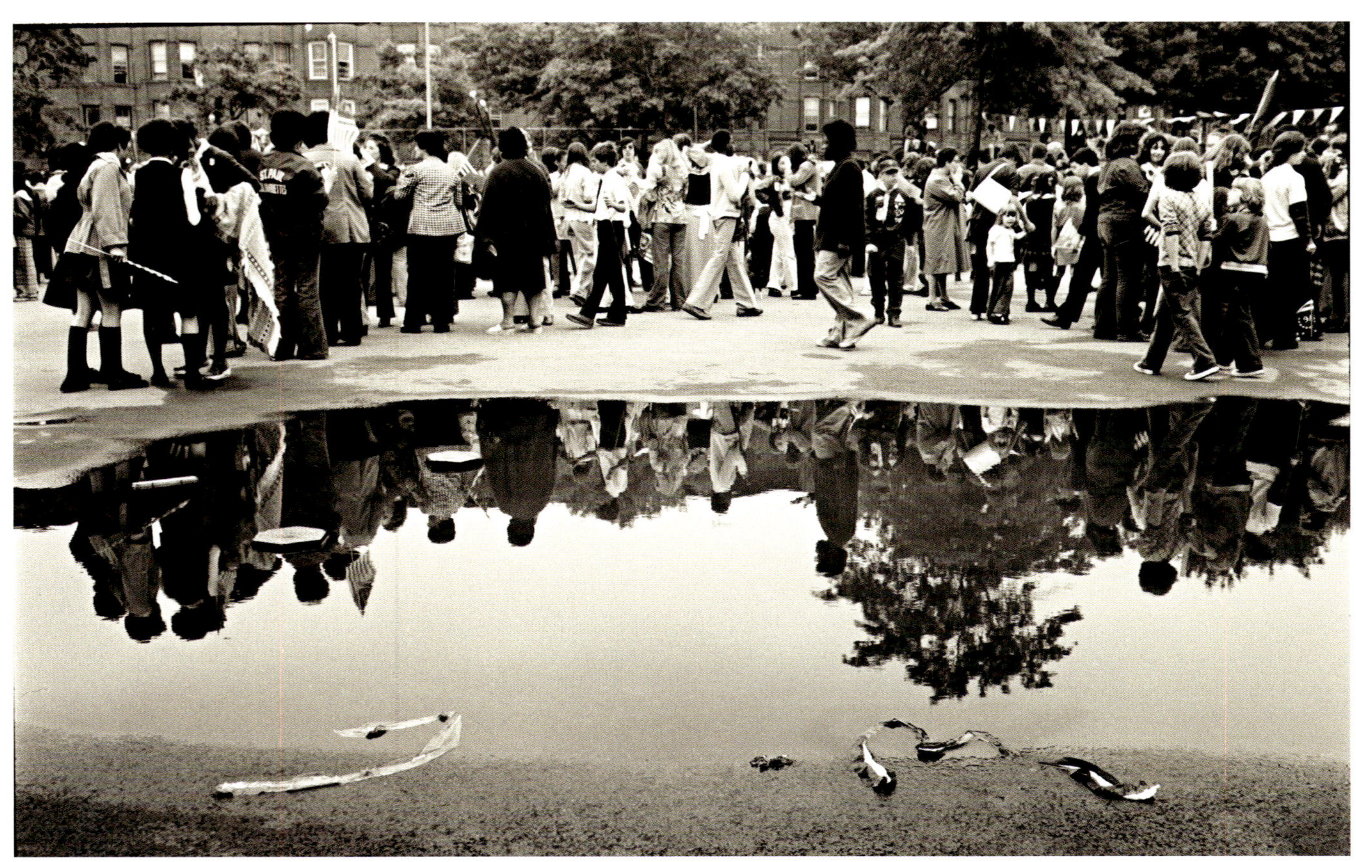

AFTERWORD, MEMORIAL DAY

Originally known as Decoration Day, Memorial Day was first commemorated in 1866 to honor all the fallen military members from Waterloo, New York, during the Civil War. Decoration Day was started by a group of women who wanted to decorate the graves of fallen soldiers with flowers, flags, and ribbons. In 1868, General John Logan called for a national Decoration Day. Through the years, Memorial Day has been expanded to include fallen military from all conflicts. In 1968, Congress included Memorial Day as one of the federal Monday holidays, and in 1971, the first "last Monday in May" Memorial Day was commemorated.

I made the photographs in this book on Memorial Day in 1976. The parade began on Twenty-Fifth Street and Fifth Avenue, across the street from the entrance to Green-Wood Cemetery. I walked ten blocks from my apartment in pre-gentrified South Brooklyn and arrived in time to see marchers and musicians warm up and tune up. Because the 200th anniversary of the signing of the Declaration of Independence would take place in the summer of 1976, this year's Memorial Day Parade was larger than usual, and included references to "America's Birthday."

As I photographed the parade, I took a slow walk through the Brooklyn I knew very well. The Italian-, Puerto Rican-, Irish- and Polish-American community members participated as both marchers and observers. They wound their way along Fifth Avenue, at some point headed up to Seventh Avenue, turned back down to Fifth and ended up at the Old Stone House Park on Fourth Street, between Fourth and Fifth Avenues. Tired marchers folded their flags, and musicians cleaned and put away their instruments. Boy Scouts and Girl Scouts, Cub Scouts and Brownies reconnected with their parents.

Eventually I moved from Brooklyn to Queens, where I have been photographing Rockaway's Memorial Day Parade for the last twenty-five years. Our parade has never been as big as that one in 1976 and has gotten smaller in recent years. Looking at my photographs spanning fifty years of Memorial Day parades, I see the passing of generations. In my recent photographs, there are fewer and fewer WWII veterans, just as WWI veterans gradually disappeared from my 1980s and 1990s photographs.

Lately I've been thinking less about the parade and more about its purpose, in relation to the meaning of all memorials and their connection to the past and our own mortality.

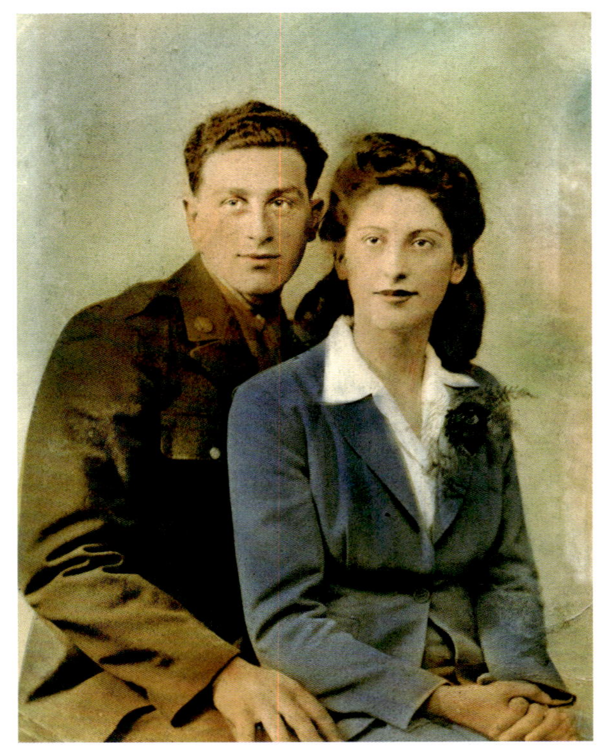

My mother and my father in his uniform, circa 1944.

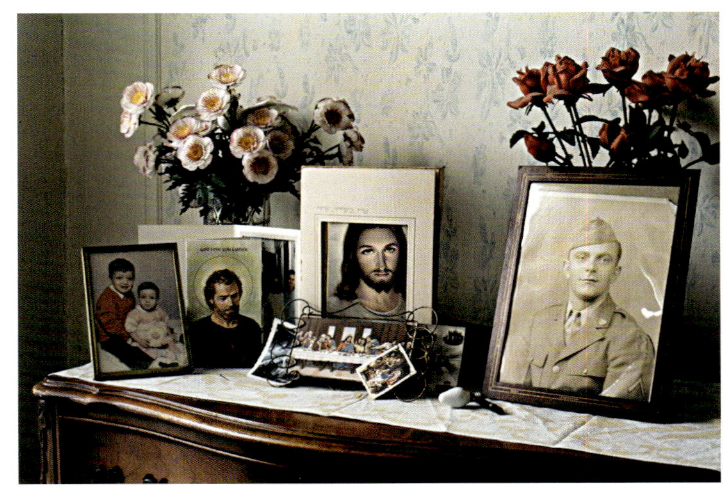

A photo of my mother's cousin on a family dresser, Brooklyn, 1975.

I have been thinking of my father, my uncles, and my father-in-law who all served during WWII. None of them are alive. Only their photographs remain, in family albums and on bedroom dressers.

Throughout New York City, there are civic and religious memorials of steel and stone honoring veterans of both World Wars. A familiar sight in many neighborhoods is the "Dough Boy" statue honoring WWI veterans.

In many local parishes, Catholic churches honor their World War II veterans by engraving their names on metal plaques or scrolls attached to religious statues near, and sometimes inside, the church.

In the 1970s, Brooklyn's George Washington VFW Post (now defunct) and the 13th Street Block Association created a simple memorial—THE ARROW CLUB. Members of this 'club" were veterans

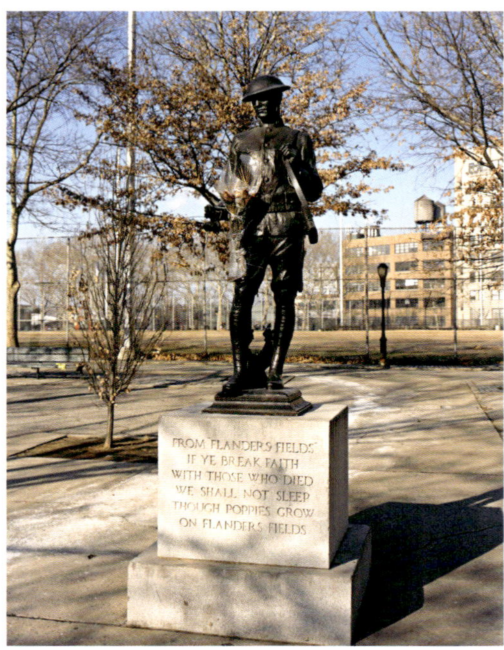

Manhattan, 2010.

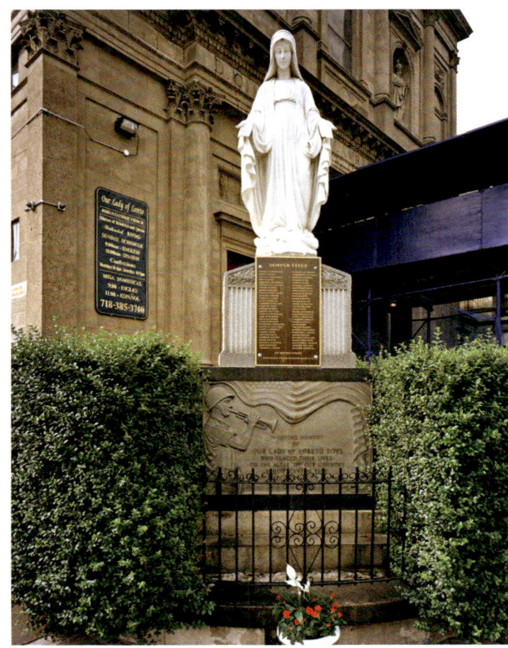

Our Lady of Loreto, Brooklyn, 2008.

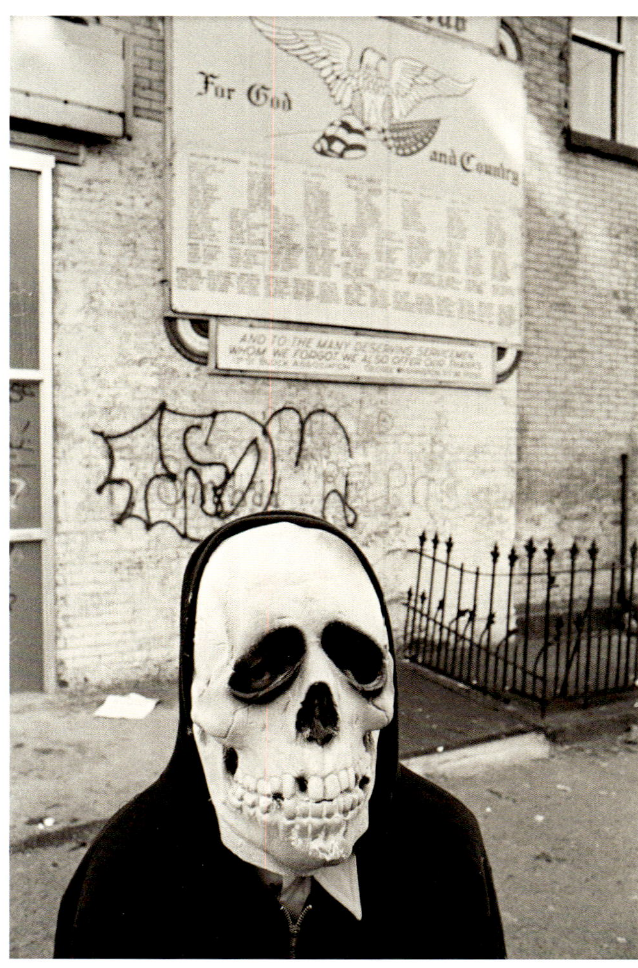

Skull mask and Arrow Club sign, Brooklyn, 1978.

of both World Wars and also Vietnam. Their names were listed on a sheet of metal attached to the side of a building at the corner of Thirteenth Street and Eighth Avenue. Although I lived only a few blocks away, I had not noticed the large sign until I photographed a masked boy in front of it one Halloween afternoon.

I hope to photograph future Memorial Day Parades, and when I do, I will keep in mind the parade's origin, and an admonition that dates back to Rudyard Kipling and the Old Testament: "Lest we forget."

Larry Racioppo

Rockaway Park, 2025

Larry Racioppo was born and raised in South Brooklyn, and he has been photographing throughout New York City since 1971. A former VISTA Volunteer and participant in the CETA Artists Project of New York City's Cultural Council Foundation, Racioppo had his first solo exhibit in 1977 at Brooklyn's F-stop Gallery, and in 1981, Scribner's published his first book of photographs, *Halloween*.

Hired in 1989 as the official photographer for the New York City Department of Housing Preservation and Development, Racioppo spent the next twenty-two years documenting the city's rebuilding of distressed neighborhoods. A Guggenheim Fellowship in 1997 enabled a yearlong leave of absence to develop personal projects, including a series of images that became *Forgotten Gateway: The Abandoned Buildings of Ellis Island*, a traveling exhibition that opened at the National Building Museum in Washington, DC.

Racioppo's photographs are in the collections of the Museum of the City of New York; the Brooklyn Museum; the New York Public Library; the Brooklyn Public Library; El Museo del Barrio, New York; and the National September 11 Memorial & Museum, New York. Recent monographs include *Brooklyn Before: Photographs, 1971–1983* (2018), *Coney Island Baby* (2021), *I Hope I Break Even, I Could Use The Money* (2024), and *Here Down On Dark Earth: Loss and Remembrance in New York City* (Fordham University Press, 2025).

Kevin Baker is a novelist, historian, and journalist, who has lived in New York since 1976, and has written extensively on the city's past and its present. His most recent book is *The New York Game: Baseball and the Rise of a New City* (2024). He is married to the playwright Ellen Abrams.

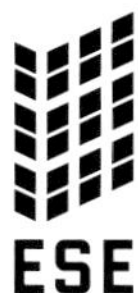

SELECT TITLES FROM EMPIRE STATE EDITIONS

Andrew J. Sparberg, *From a Nickel to a Token: The Journey from Board of Transportation to MTA*

Daniel Campo, *The Accidental Playground: Brooklyn Waterfront Narratives of the Undesigned and Unplanned*

Gerard R. Wolfe, *The Synagogues of New York's Lower East Side: A Retrospective and Contemporary View, Second Edition.* Photographs by Jo Renée Fine and Norman Borden, Foreword by Joseph Berger

Joseph B. Raskin, *The Routes Not Taken: A Trip Through New York City's Unbuilt Subway System*

Phillip Deery, *Red Apple: Communism and McCarthyism in Cold War New York*

North Brother Island: The Last Unknown Place in New York City. Photographs by Christopher Payne, A History by Randall Mason, Essay by Robert Sullivan

Stephen Miller, *Walking New York: Reflections of American Writers from Walt Whitman to Teju Cole*

Dorothy Day and the Catholic Worker: The Miracle of Our Continuance. Edited, with an Introduction and Additional Text by Kate Hennessy, Photographs by Vivian Cherry, Text by Dorothy Day

Mark Naison and Bob Gumbs, *Before the Fires: An Oral History of African American Life in the Bronx from the 1930s to the 1960s*

Robert Weldon Whalen, *Murder, Inc., and the Moral Life: Gangsters and Gangbusters in La Guardia's New York*

Joanne Witty and Henrik Krogius, *Brooklyn Bridge Park: A Dying Waterfront Transformed*

Sharon Egretta Sutton, *When Ivory Towers Were Black: A Story about Race in America's Cities and Universities*

Pamela Hanlon, *A Wordly Affair: New York, the United Nations, and the Story Behind Their Unlikely Bond*

Britt Haas, *Fighting Authoritarianism: American Youth Activism in the 1930s*

David J. Goodwin, *Left Bank of the Hudson: Jersey City and the Artists of 111 1st Street.* Foreword by DW Gibson

Nandini Bagchee, *Counter Institution: Activist Estates of the Lower East Side*

Susan Celia Greenfield (ed.), *Sacred Shelter: Thirteen Journeys of Homelessness and Healing*

Elizabeth Macaulay-Lewis and Matthew M. McGowan (eds.), *Classical New York: Discovering Greece and Rome in Gotham*

Susan Opotow and Zachary Baron Shemtob (eds.), *New York after 9/11*

Andrew Feffer, *Bad Faith: Teachers, Liberalism, and the Origins of McCarthyism*

Colin Davey with Thomas A. Lesser, *The American Museum of Natural History and How It Got That Way.* Forewords by Neil deGrasse Tyson and Kermit Roosevelt III

Wendy Jean Katz, *Humbug: The Politics of Art Criticism in New York City's Penny Press*

Mike Jaccarino, *America's Last Great Newspaper War: The Death of Print in a Two-Tabloid Town*

Angel Garcia, *The Kingdom Began in Puerto Rico: Neil Connolly's Priesthood in the South Bronx*

Jim Mackin, *Notable New Yorkers of Manhattan's Upper West Side: Bloomingdale–Morningside Heights*

Matthew Spady, *The Neighborhood Manhattan Forgot: Audubon Park and the Families Who Shaped It*

Robert O. Binnewies, *Palisades: 100,000 Acres in 100 Years*

Marilyn S. Greenwald and Yun Li, *Eunice Hunton Carter: A Lifelong Fight for Social Justice*

Jeffrey A. Kroessler, *Sunnyside Gardens: Planning and Preservation in a Historic Garden Suburb*

Elizabeth Macaulay-Lewis, *Antiquity in Gotham: The Ancient Architecture of New York City*

Ron Howell, *King Al: How Sharpton Took the Throne*

Jean Arrington with Cynthia S. LaValle, *From Factories to Palaces: Architect Charles B. J. Snyder and the New York City Public Schools.* Foreword by Peg Breen

Boukary Sawadogo, *Africans in Harlem: An Untold New York Story*

Alvin Eng, *Our Laundry, Our Town: My Chinese American Life from Flushing to the Downtown Stage and Beyond*

Stephanie Azzarone, *Heaven on the Hudson: Mansions, Monuments, and Marvels of Riverside Park*

Ron Goldberg, *Boy with the Bullhorn: A Memoir and History of ACT UP New York*. Foreword by Dan Barry

Peter Quinn, *Cross Bronx: A Writing Life*

Mark Bulik, *Ambush at Central Park: When the IRA Came to New York*

Matt Dallos, *In the Adirondacks: Dispatches from the Largest Park in the Lower 48*

Brandon Dean Lamson, *Caged: A Teacher's Journey Through Rikers, or How I Beheaded the Minotaur*

Raj Tawney, *Colorful Palate: Savored Stories from a Mixed Life*

Edward Cahill, *Disorderly Men*

Joseph Heathcott, *Global Queens: An Urban Mosaic*

Francis R. Kowsky with Lucille Gordon, *Hell on Color, Sweet on Song: Jacob Wrey Mould and the Artful Beauty of Central Park*

Jill Jonnes, *South Bronx Rising: The Rise, Fall, and Resurrection of an American City, Third Edition*

Barbara G. Mensch, *A Falling-Off Place: The Transformation of Lower Manhattan*

David J. Goodwin, *Midnight Rambles: H. P. Lovecraft in Gotham*

Felipe Luciano, *Flesh and Spirit: Confessions of a Young Lord*

Jennifer Baum, *Just City: Growing Up on the Upper West Side When Housing Was a Human Right*

Davida Siwisa James, *Hamilton Heights and Sugar Hill: Alexander Hamilton's Old Harlem Neighborhood Through the Centuries*

Annik LaFarge, *On the High Line: The Definitive Guide, Third Edition*. Foreword by Rick Dark

Marie Carter, *Mortimer and the Witches: A History of Nineteenth-Century Fortune Tellers*

Alice Sparberg Alexiou, *Devil's Mile: The Rich, Gritty History of the Bowery*. Foreword by Peter Quinn

Carey Kasten and Brenna Moore, *Mutuality in El Barrio: Stories of the Little Sisters of the Assumption Family Health Service*. Foreword by Norma Benítez Sánchez

Kimberly A. Orcutt, *The American Art-Union: Utopia and Skepticism in the Antebellum Era*

Jonathan Butler, *Join the Conspiracy: How a Brooklyn Eccentric Got Lost on the Right, Infiltrated the Left, and Brought Down the Biggest Bombing Network in New York*

Nicole Gelinas, *Movement: New York's Long War to Take Back Its Streets from the Car*

Jack Hodgson, *Young Reds in the Big Apple: The New York Young Pioneers of America, 1923–1934*

Lynn Ellsworth, *Wonder City: How to Reclaim Human-Scale Urban Life*

Walter Zev Feldman, *From the Bronx to the Bosphorus: Klezmer and Other Displaced Musics of New York*

Larry Racioppo, *Here Down on Dark Earth: Loss and Remembrance in New York City*

Bonnie Yochelson, *Too Good to Get Married: The Life and Photographs of Miss Alice Austen*

David Brown Morris, *Ten Thousand Central Parks: A Climate-Change Parable*

Eve M. Kahn, *Queen of Bohemia Predicts Own Death: The Forgotten Journalist Zoe Anderson Norris, 1860-1914*

Miriam Chaiken, *Creative Ozone: The Artists of Westbeth*

Stefanie Mercado Altman, Claire Altman, and Stan Altman, *Twice Blessed: A Story of Unconditional Love*. Foreword by Stephen G. Post

Stephanie Azzarone, *Fabulous Fountains of New York*

Annik LaFarge, *Composing Olana: A Journey on Foot Through an American Landscape*

Phyllis Ross, *Stories in Fabric: The Design Works of Bedford Stuyvesant*. Foreword by Judith Jones

Paul Schmitz, *New York's Family Grocer: The Story of D'Agostino Supermarkets*

For a complete list, visit www.fordhampress.com/empire-state-editions.